The Winding Road

A Journey of Survival

Miriam Hurdle

Library of Congress Control Number: 2022912457

Cover Image: Pixabay
Cover Design: Miriam Hurdle
ISBN: 9798842330812, Paperback (B&W)

Printed in the United State of America

For

my caring husband Lynton
and
my loving daughter Mercy
and
my granddaughters Autumn & Nora
and
their offspring

Contents

Foreword

You know the ending before you read the story because I'm here to tell it to you. My path was long and dark, but I survived. The ending is an important part of a story, but the journey gives it meaning. At many points during this cancer treatment, I felt death was teasing me. I lost most of my muscle mass, 20% of my blood, and almost all of my energy. Yet, I was breathing. It caused me to ponder. What is life?

Life is a gift. It is precious, and it's worth fighting for. If I died, my pain went with me, but I would leave pain with my loved ones. My life is worth living.

I had an active and productive life until the point when I had cancer. When I couldn't lift my feet to walk, being productive was thousands of miles away from my thoughts. My family became the only value in my life.

I fought for my life, but not alone. My family and friends were alongside me. In fact, they carried me through this uphill battle.

I want to live to appreciate the beauty of the earth, and everything that lives on it, and to enjoy the loving relationships among my family and friends.

I'm grateful to be alive, to give to others, and to receive from them.

Chapter 1

Cancer Discovery

July 2008

My hysterectomy surgery was on July 31, 2008. Schools didn't start until the first week of September. It would give me two to three weeks to recover before returning to work.

On the morning of the operation, my husband, Lynton, drove me to St. Jude Medical Center, which was three miles from my home. After checking in, he stayed with me until the patient transport specialist wheeled me to the operating room. The surgical team members lifted me from the gurney onto the operating table. The anesthesiologist called my name and introduced himself to me. He said Dr. Gray was on the way. Immediately after nodding, the anesthesia rendered me unconscious.

I woke up in my hospital room in the afternoon. *There was no pain in my abdomen. Perhaps the anesthesia had not worn off yet.* Outside the window were familiar buildings. One of them was the new imaging center. The medical center completed a new patient care building adjacent to the existing one. My private room was on the third floor of the new building. I had driven up and down the streets in this area and watched this being built. I felt strange being inside it.

Lynton came with a bouquet at the same time I woke up. He stayed with me until dinner time and said he would call me early in the morning. It was a relief that the fibroids I had for years were out for good.

At 10:00 p.m., Dr. Gray came to the room and greeted me with a smile. I returned a smile with apprehension. Doctors didn't visit patients late at night unless there was an emergency. He sat down by the bed. "The surgery went well," he said, "and I wanted to share the pathology result with you."

My puzzlement grew, but I nodded and kept a polite smile.

"The pathology result shows that the mass in your female organ was melanoma. I've never seen it before, so I did some research. The research shows that melanoma is the most aggressive, invasive, and dangerous cancer."

He detected the perplexity on my face, and said, "It looks like it's in stage I or II, the beginning stage. Cancer has not spread into other parts of the body yet."

I wanted to ask questions, but my mind went blank. *What questions could I ask? Where would I begin?* Moisture saturated my eyes.

"I have lined up the referrals for you to see specialists for treatment. Call my cell phone if you have questions. I start my vacation tomorrow." He handed me a note with his phone number.

"But you'll be on vacation," I said, still trying to find words.

"That's what a cell phone is for." he smiled. "I'm glad God put you in my care."

His visit left me puzzled.

~ ~ ~

The next day, I still had no pain, even though the anesthesia had worn off.

Lynton called me around 9:00 a.m. to let me know he was coming to see me later that day. He told me his dad had passed away. He was on the phone with his siblings before he called. His dad had been at Loma Linda University Medical Center ICU since the previous Wednesday after having a heart attack and kidney infection. The infection went into his bloodstream and his condition worsened. After the infection was cured, he was on dialysis to give his kidneys a break and to see if he improved. Lynton and I went to see him after he was transferred to the patient care unit. He was unconscious when we got there. The entire family of twelve was there talking to each other about the latest progress. Lynton's dad heard our voices and opened his eyes. We went close to his bedside to hold his hands and speak to him. His eyes sparkled a little, and then he lost consciousness again. That was the last time I saw him alive.

I asked Lynton, "Would you ask your family to schedule the funeral service after I get home from the hospital? I want to attend the service."

"Don't worry. My family will consider that when they plan for the funeral service," he said. "I'm on my way to the hospital to see you."

When he arrived, I gave him the news. He faced me with a brooding look. "I will research melanoma as soon as I get home," he said. He told me his siblings had arranged a family-only, private graveside service for his dad on Friday, August 8th at the Montecito Cemetery in Riverside.

"That's good. I have a week to rest before going to the service." I was relieved by the arrangement.

The nurse came in to check on me. "How are you feeling?"

"I'm feeling very well, with no pain. Can I go home today?"

"The attending doctor is not here yet. Let me check your incision and change the dressing. I'll let the doctor know about your condition. He has to authorize the discharge."

The doctor came in an hour later. After checking my progress, he authorized the discharge.

"Thank you, doctor," I said to him while my mind spun at record speed, miles into the search engine, chasing the meaning of melanoma.

What if there was no hysterectomy? How would I have found out about melanoma? There was no pain or any warning symptoms. I'm grateful for the hysterectomy.

~ ~ ~

A few months ago, in April of the same year, I met with my family physician, Dr. Royce Hutain, for an annual pap smear. He had been my family doctor since the 1990s.

I checked in at the doctor's private office and sat in the waiting room. Dr. Hutain's wife had helped to decorate the waiting room. The figurines in the curio at one corner resembled home decorations. She chose lavender, purple, and wintergreen as the color scheme. They were my favorite colors. Outside of a floor-to-ceiling glass window, and at the same height, was a six-foot deep bird cage with a screen cover. My favorite bird was the colorful parakeet. Ample magazines were in several places around the room. I grabbed two and started reading.

"Elston Hurdle," the nurse announced.

"Yes." My gaze reached hers as I returned the magazines to the table.

"This way, please. The doctor will be in momentarily. Put the gown on with the opening in the back. Press the green light when you're ready." She closed the door behind her.

Shortly after I pressed the green light, Dr. Hutain knocked, then came in. The pap smear procedure took just a few minutes.

"The fibroid is eleven centimeters. It was seven centimeters last year," he said. "You had an operation to remove the fibroids twenty years ago. One fibroid grew back to seven centimeters when I checked last year, but it has enlarged by four centimeters within one year. Something is going on. Let me refer you to the gynecologist. Janet will submit the referral to the insurance."

"Thank you, Doctor."

It didn't worry me because uterine fibroids are noncancerous. Many women have them during their lives. They might not know it because the fibroids often cause no symptoms. I didn't feel any pain during those twenty years.

~ ~ ~

I was at my gynecologist Dr. Brian Gray's office six weeks after the referral because the insurance required authorization for the visit.

The nurse called and took me into the examination room. After Dr. Gray asked me a few routine questions, his nurse came in to assist him. The nurse handed him tools to examine my vagina. Next, he put both hands, one on top of another, to apply a little pressure on my abdomen. He then checked any lumps in my breasts. After that, he extended a bent elbow to me. I grabbed it to pull my body upright with my legs dangling on the examination table.

He scooted his stool backward against the corner of the room and looked at me.

"Yes, the fibroid is eleven centimeters, four centimeters larger than last year." Dr. Gray concurred with Dr. Hutain's finding.

"I felt nothing. What caused it to grow so fast suddenly?" I tried to understand.

"Not all women with fibroids have symptoms. We don't know what causes them to grow rapidly. We only know hormones affect them. Hormones might have fed into the growth, but we are not sure. I think it's time for a hysterectomy to remove the uterus, to eliminate any future problems. I'll operate using the same incision site from your C-section, so you won't have additional scars."

"Thank you, Doctor," I said with no worries.

After the doctor's visit, I made an appointment for hysterectomy surgery on July 31st. I've had many operations in my life. This is just one more.

~ ~ ~

Here I am in the hospital the day after the operation. The news about melanoma came to me as a shock. This hysterectomy surgery was not "just one more!"

Chapter 2

Research on Melanoma

August 2008

The day after I came home from the hospital, my abdomen was not too painful. It was numb with thick scarred tissues from the three surgeries-the C-section, the first surgery to remove the initial fibroids, and this one. I had no strength to prop up my body. Using my previous experience, I rolled my body to the right side, extended my legs out of bed onto the floor, and used my elbow to push myself up. I moved around slowly and tried to wake up my brain. The research was on my mind.

Lynton and I researched melanoma in the internal organs, especially in the female organs.

What is melanoma? How much longer do I live? These were my ultimate questions. With swirling thoughts, I chased keywords on the internet such as stages, prognosis, treatment, and survival rates. I knew melanoma was a serious type of skin cancer in the visible skin areas, but I didn't know it could be in the internal organ, such as the intestines.

I didn't know many people who had melanoma. Cancer wasn't a topic of social discussion.

My findings showed melanoma makes up the smallest percentage of all skin cancers, but it is dangerous because it can spread to different parts of the body. At stage 0, cancer is in the epidermis and hasn't spread. At stages I through IV, it is invasive and can spread to other areas. Cancer is well-localized at stages I and II and has a very successful treatment rate. By stages III and IV, it has spread to the lymph nodes and could spread to other organs, such as the lungs, liver, and bone. The higher the number, the lower the chances of a full recovery.

In 2007, melanoma in the female organ had less than 300 cases reported worldwide. Metastatic melanomas were even rarer and only five cases were reported. Those cases were found in postmenopausal females between 57 to 75 years old.

The research only told me I had an exceedingly rare cancer, and I was among the age group of women who got it. The factors contributing to it were unknown.

My only hope was Dr. Gray's treatment referral would go through quickly to have the cancerous cells removed before they spread. In the meantime, all I could do was wait. I pressed my hands on my abdomen and prayed, and asked God to contain cancer in a local area.

I'm grateful for the early discovery of cancer through my hysterectomy. I didn't have any pain, and there was no warning. It could have developed into an advanced stage and spread to my organs and brain. I hope that early treatment will eliminate the threat to my body and my life.

I checked the school district website to find out when teachers could start setting up their classrooms. It would be my first day returning to the classroom after ten years of district administration. It was an understatement to say I felt anxious and stressed.

Chapter 3

Job Assignment Change

March 2008

Back in March this year, I was sitting in my quiet office. Schools were busy testing students, so there were few teachers or school staff coming in and out of our office.

The school district superintendent called me. I had a strange feeling about the call. We had a management meeting last Wednesday, and there was no sign she needed to talk to me about anything.

"Miriam, I would like to see you at two o'clock this afternoon. Or would you like to come this morning?" she said.

"I could come right now if it's okay."

"Sure, please come."

I dropped everything and headed out of my office. Our office was in a satellite location with a large conference room for teacher training and parent meetings. The main district office was half a mile away. Occasionally, the business manager, the secretary, and I walked there and back on our lunch break. On this day, I zipped over there, parked the car, and walked into her office wondering what it was all about.

"I'm here to see Jonnie, Rosa," I said to the administrative assistant. The superintendent wanted to go on a first-name basis.

"She is expecting you."

The door had opened a crack. I knocked.

"Please come in."

"Good morning, Jonnie."

"Please sit." Her hand gestured to a side seat next to a long table. She then sat down near the end of the table.

Her office has a large desk and a long table used as a workstation or for small group meetings, such as cabinet meetings. I sat in the same seat many times, working with the previous two superintendents on different projects. Jonnie had never asked me to work on any special projects. Perhaps she was more comfortable with a couple of administrators whom she worked with when she was a principal.

The previous two superintendents assigned me to work on many special programs. My mind went down memory lane for a few seconds.

Dr. Davis was my field supervisor when I did the doctoral program at the University of La Verne. He took me under his wings for three years and delegated me to work on special assignments to fulfill my course requirements. After he retired, Dr. Lowe from Human Resources and Jonnie from the Curriculum Department applied for the job. The school board recommended Dr. Lowe because he had a doctorate degree. Jonnie was mad. She went to work for the County of Education on loan for two years. She could come back to the district anytime without losing her seniority at the district. Rumor had it that she met with her district friends periodically to update the ins and outs of the district. Dr. Lowe sent me to a Strategic Planning Conference. When I came back, I headed up the districtwide strategic planning involving all levels of school staff, parents, and community leaders. When Dr. Lowe left, Jonnie applied for the job and was hired.

Here I was, at her office. She looked at me with a smile, trying to ease the tension of the conversation. "As you know, the district has declining enrollments three years in a row. The cabinet recommended dismissing twelve teachers. Each school will cut one or two classes next year. Some administrators and resource teachers will be assigned to the classroom. We may send you back to the classroom next year, but we'll know before the school year is over."

"I understand, Jonnie. The number of ESL students and Title I students has reduced in the last few years."

"That's the situation. We're losing the federal and state funds. I just let you know now, and I'll try to keep your position as much as I could."

"Thank you, Jonnie."

On my way back to our office, I couldn't help but ask, "Why me?"

It crossed my mind she was resentful that I worked closely with the previous superintendents. *Dr. Lowe got the superintendent's job because he had a doctorate degree. Did my doctorate degree make her uncomfortable? Why did she pick on me now? I would never find out the answer.*

Our department, the Integrated Programs Office, oversaw the programs for English Learners or ESL students and Title 1 students of low-income families. We were in charge of the federal and state funds generated from these student populations. Losing students would cause less funding for the student programs and the support of the staff in our department. Perhaps the reduced funding resulted in cutting my position.

After meeting with the superintendent, I couldn't concentrate on doing anything that afternoon. My mind was frozen. I felt disappointed because the changes interrupted my plan. I taught in the classroom for thirteen years and was in administration for ten. Three years prior, I started planning to retire after 25 years of education. By this time, I needed to work for two more years before retirement. A principal who retired the previous year purchased a five-year service credit to maximize the retirement benefit from the State Teacher Retirement System (STRS). She worked for twenty-five years and bought five years of service credit. She retired with thirty years of service.

I wanted to follow the same strategy, so I signed up to purchase five years of service credit. The payment was high, but I could afford it with my administrative salary. The total payment was $190,000, equivalent to the amount the school district paid for my retirement, plus my contributions for five years. When I signed up three years prior, I paid a lump sum of $90,000 with a monthly deduction for the following five years. I had two more years to pay for my purchase.

That was my plan. It was a perfect plan.

~ ~ ~

When I got back to my office, my supervisor was in a meeting. I waited until the next day to talk to her. She said the budget committee recommended changing my job assignment. My head was spinning with the news.

I don't know how to pray about this assignment change. Have I done anything wrong to anyone to deserve this? There are only two more years before my retirement. I wish to stay at my job for the remainder of the time. But I don't know what God has in mind for me. I'll keep this between God and me in the meantime. He has always answered my prayers, whether it was a "yes" or "no."

For a while I had a tiny hope, but not too much. I started cleaning up my office and organizing my computer files. I also packed my personal things to take home a little at a time.

Well, during the last week of school, the superintendent confirmed she reassigned me to a classroom position. My heart sank.

"The ESL student testing should have been done by now. I hope the teachers turn in the progress reports as soon as possible," my supervisor said.

"Most of the teachers turned them in already, but there are a few who will wait until the last day of school to do it."

"This is your regular summer project to scan the student testing results and prepare the new cards for the teachers next year to mark the learning progress. How long do you think you need to do it?"

"Six weeks is about right. I can finish by July 30th," I said.

~ ~ ~

When Dr. Gray told me I needed to have the hysterectomy, I scheduled the surgery for July 31st.

It would be hard to step into the classroom again. Teaching at a young age and easing eventually into retirement is manageable. Starting to teach at retirement age would be a different story as far as meeting the physical and mental demands. There were a lot of changes in the past ten years.

The district just adopted new reading textbooks. There were so many new things to learn about teaching. It was like going into a brand-new job.

Anyway, I needed to work. Lynton's business didn't do well. He applied to go back to school to get the CT/MRI licenses. Loma Linda University accepted him, and his first semester would start in September. He would take classes all day on one day and have internship work for four days. It eased my anxiety, knowing I had a job and health insurance even though it was not my preference to return to the classroom.

Chapter 4

Back to the Classroom

August 2008

The new school year began in early September for students, but the school facility was open for the principals and secretaries in the middle of August. This allowed the parents from the community to enroll their children in school. The secretary posted the class lists on the bulletin board in the hallway next to the office. Parents of the returning students came to find out about the room numbers and teachers for their children.

Teachers could start setting up their classrooms and check out their class lists. The class lists and the student testing results from the previous year would help the teachers to make learning plans for the students.

My school assignment was a Kindergarten/first-grade combination at Parkway school. Away from the classroom for ten years, just thinking of handling tiny kids was overwhelming to me. I had nine kindergarten students and eleven first-grade students. The district implemented small class sizes for kindergarten to third grade with less than twenty-five students in each class.

"The number of students is not final yet. We still have new enrollments coming in. If I have enough students to add another kindergarten class, you may have a different grade level," the principal said.

"I understand, Ms. Powell. In the meantime, I'll set up the classroom for the grade levels you gave me."

My previous experience told me the class assignments could be different in the first two weeks of school. Lynton helped me set up half of the classroom with smaller tables and chairs for kindergarten and half for first grade. We covered the bulletin board with colored butcher paper and displayed greeting messages and some generic grade-level posters.

The custodian was busy moving student tables and chairs when class configurations changed. He understood he had to move them again when the numbers changed. He stacked up some smaller chairs and put them in a corner. They would be there if my classroom would become a full-size kindergarten class.

We had an open house the first week of school. Most of my parents came. They were enthusiastic about introducing themselves to me and told me what their children did in the summer. Many parents were interested in knowing what their children would be learning in my class. Meeting with the parents helped me to feel excited to be back in the classroom.

Usually, the kindergarten students were shy, trying to adjust to the new learning environment. There was a little blond, curly hair girl, Serina, who was cute but uncontrollable. She ran around and around the classroom and climbed up and down the stacked-up chairs. My teacher's assistant chased her all over the class but couldn't settle her down. I had yard duty that week. A third grader came to tell me that Serina locked herself in the stall in the girl's restroom and didn't want to come out. I asked the girl to report to the principal because I couldn't leave my yard duty.

By the end of the first week, my body was exhausted. Even though there was no pain from the hysterectomy surgery, I was not fully recovered yet. The idea of retirement had never sounded sweeter. But not just yet. I needed the job, and the health insurance, especially this year.

Two weeks into school in September, the school had enough students to add one more kindergarten class. Ms. Powell adjusted the student numbers in kindergarten to second-grade classes. She let me know I got a first/second-grade combination class. I felt a lot better because the students were older and were more independent in the classroom activities.

The teachers were friendly. I worked with most of them on unique occasions, such as staff training, grade level development, and student testing.

"We have a new textbook adoption this year. We are learning how to use the textbooks the same way you do." The second-grade teachers told me after the staff meeting in the second week of school.

"I may have to borrow many teaching resources from you before spending too much money," I said to one teacher.

"Come to my classroom after school and let me know what you need." The teacher offered.

I felt welcomed by the teachers and appreciated their support.

Chapter 5

Surgery at UCLA

August to October 2008

Dr. Gray mentioned two choices of hospitals for my surgery. I preferred UC Irvine Medical Center because it's close to home, but my health insurance didn't cover it. He then referred me to the UCLA Medical Center in Los Angeles. The insurance approved it on August 18th.

My appointment with Dr. Eisner at the UCLA Medical Center was on August 25th. He confirmed our research that melanoma is the most dangerous, aggressive, and invasive cancer. Metastatic cancer spreads randomly. It could go into the bloodstream and invade the organ and the brain. He told us his plan was to have the surgery and then have the chemotherapy and radiation afterward. He ordered the CT/PET scan to check the progress of my cancer.

My next appointment with Dr. Eisner was on September 15th to review the CT/PET scan results. He compared the scan results to those taken three months ago before my hysterectomy. The report showed cancer had gone to the inguinal lymph nodes in my right groin area. It had progressed from stage I or II to stage III. It meant that cancer might continue spreading to other body parts through the lymphatic system.

He scheduled the operation for October 16th.

Oh no, my cancer is spreading. It's true that melanoma spreads fast. I still must wait for an entire month before the surgery. How fast will the cancer spread during this month? Will it spread to my brain before the operation?

I'm not afraid of dying. I'll just stop all the pain and move on to the next world. My concerns are Lynton and Mercy. Lynton said he has loved no one else the way he loves me. He'll be devastated to lose me. As for Mercy, her dad took her away from me for five years with almost no contact. I saw her once the second year after they moved away. Mercy and I reunited two years ago. We just started getting to know each other. I want to spend more time with Mercy, watch her get married, and have kids. It will be a great joy to babysit my grandchildren. I know everyone dies, but I just want to spend more time with Lynton and Mercy.

I took two weeks off from school in October for the operation and the time needed for the recovery. I only went back to the classroom for six weeks and needed to take two weeks off already. Somehow, it was easier to take time off as a teacher. All I had to do was to request a substitute teacher.

Had I stayed in my district office position, it would be harder for someone to fill in during my absence.

On October 15th, I came home from school and packed my bag. Lynton came home at 10:00 p.m., an hour earlier from his afternoon shift at the CT/MRI job. We went to bed at midnight and got four hours of sleep before heading to the Medical Center.

The next day, we arrived at UCLA Medical Center at 6:00 a.m. and checked in at the admission office. The admission staff didn't know where we should go. She said she would locate my operating room and told us to wait in the Pre-Operative Holding Area. A nurse asked me to change into a hospital gown and took my vital signs.

We waited for two hours. Finally, someone came to look for us. It was the nuclear medicine doctor and her intern. She said she called the admission office and paged us for two hours. She said I needed to have an X-ray with a dye injection before the surgery. The dye would travel to show the contrast between the normal and cancerous cells for the doctor to perform the operation. She was not sure if the X-ray technician was available since I missed the scheduled time. If the X-ray wasn't done, she had to postpone the surgery. She called the imaging center and told us the X-ray technician was available for me. I was relieved that the operation was on schedule.

Lynton kissed me and said a prayer for me before the patient transport specialist wheeled me to the operating room. Two operation team members greeted me. They asked if I could scoot from the gurney onto the operating table. I did it with little effort. The anesthesiologist greeted me and injected the anesthetic into the back of my left hand. He told me Dr. Eisner was on the way. In an instant, his face faded away.

It was late in the afternoon when I woke up in my private hospital room. I was groggy but didn't feel any pain in my abdomen. There was an IV inserted into my left arm. I felt small dressing pads on my abdomen.

The nurse came in and logged on to the computer.

"Dr. Eisner took six hours to complete your operation," she said. "He'll prepare a surgery report for you when you check out. Here's the dinner menu. You can order your dinner."

"I'm not hungry, but I'll order something light for dinner. I don't feel any pain. How long will I stay?"

"You may feel the pain after the anesthetic wears off. Try to eat something and drink as much water as you can. You must pass urine before the doctor discharges you. I'll check on you after dinner."

The next day, I had no pain when the doctor checked on me, so he discharged me. After we arrived home, Lynton and I read the discharge report. Dr. Eisner did a laparoscopic operation, which is a robotic-assisted procedure, by making several small incisions in the lower abdomen to insert the tools. He placed a laparoscope, which is a lighted tube with a tiny camera through one incision, and through the remaining incisions, he inserted small surgical tools to remove cancerous tissues. The discharge report showed Dr. Eisner did the operation at six spots. After the initial procedure, he did a biopsy. The margins were not clear in one spot. He removed additional tissue from that area.

The follow-up meeting with Dr. Eisner was a few days later. After going over the surgery results with us, he said the Tumor Board at UCLA recommended chemotherapy and radiation, which should start within six weeks after the operation. He referred me back to my primary care physician at St. Jude Medical Center, to follow up on the recommendation.

Chapter 6

Referral for Chemotherapy

October 2008

I took Dr. Eisner's chemotherapy recommendation to the oncology department at St. Jude and gave it to the receptionist. She said she would call me after the doctor reviewed it.

One week went by and I didn't receive any phone call. There were five weeks left before I should have started the chemo. I called the doctor's office. The receptionist said there was no news for me and that she would call me later. I waited, called again, waited, and called again, but there was no news.

Three weeks had gone by. I was still waiting. The Medical Center was three miles from home. It was quicker to drive there than to wait for the phone call, so I did.

"I brought a referral for the chemotherapy three weeks ago. When can I see the doctor?" I spoke to the receptionist.

She reached into the doctor's inbox. "The referral is here. He has done nothing yet."

"I should start the chemo soon. Can I talk to the doctor?"

"I don't know. He is not here today. The paper is in his box." She had no interest in finding out more about how to help me. She was laughing and chit-chatting with another receptionist. I didn't want to leave the office. I could wait forever if I just went home.

I stayed in the waiting room and refused to leave. After half an hour, a lady came to see me. She said she was a home care nurse.

"I'm dying. I have melanoma. I had surgery at UCLA. The surgeon referred me back to St. Jude for chemotherapy within six weeks after the surgery. It has been three weeks. The referral is in your doctor's inbox, untouched."

"I will call the Case Management Supervisor in the morning. She'll get in touch with you. Call me if you don't hear from her tomorrow." She handed me her business card.

I thanked her and went home.

The next day, the Case Management Supervisor, Diana Stinson, called me and set up an appointment for me with Dr. Panera.

A few days later, I was at Dr. Panera's office. He said, "I've never seen melanoma in a female organ. I read Dr. Eisner's report. The report showed that he found one cancerous lymph node, but he didn't remove it. In fact, I talked with him on the phone yesterday. He said the Tumor Board recommended treating it five days a week for twenty-six weeks with chemotherapy. The chemotherapy at St. Jude uses a single drug, Interferon Alpha, to treat general melanoma. There is no specific treatment for your condition."

"But Dr. Eisner referred me back here for chemotherapy." I didn't take "no" for an answer.

"We have nothing specific for you at St. Jude." He responded.

What can I do? I was horrified. *How can a doctor say such a thing to a cancer patient? Is this the end of the road?*

"I can make a referral. Dr. Steven O'Day at The Angeles Clinic and Research Institute was my oncology internship supervisor. He is a melanoma specialist, one of the two top specialists in the US. I want you to see him." He called to set up an appointment for me while I was in his office.

Chapter 7

Experimental Treatment Recommendation

November 2008

My appointment with Dr. O'Day was on November 25th, during Thanksgiving week. I took Monday through Wednesday off. The school had Thursday and Friday as holidays.

Mercy arrived from Portland, Oregon on Saturday, November 22nd, my birthday, to spend a week with us. It was a treat for me. She came to celebrate my birthday. We went to a local Italian restaurant for dinner. She had become a vegetarian a few years ago and was glad she had many choices of dishes.

The next day, Mercy went with us to our adult fellowship class at church. Most of the people in this class knew her since she was six, but they hadn't seen her for many years.

I reintroduced her, "This is my daughter Mercy. She is here to spend Thanksgiving week with us. Thank you for praying for me. I'll be meeting with a new doctor on Tuesday. I pray I'll live long enough to see her getting... married... and have kids." My voice choked with tears in my eyes.

"Don't push." Dr. Lampman burst out in humor. The class laughed. It lightened the tension in my sadness. Dr. Lampman was a high school teacher at Sunny Hills where Mercy went for two years before moving to Oregon with her dad. His wife Fran babysat Mercy once when she was little. I was grateful for this class as my extended family.

On Tuesday, November 25th, Lynton took me to the 4:30 p.m. appointment. It was the first appointment available when Dr. Panera called The Angeles Clinic and Research Institute. The office was in Los Angeles by the Interstate 10 freeway and 405 freeway. The after-work traffic was bumper to bumper. When we got to the LAX airport area, the traffic came to a halt. I called Dr. O'Day's office. He said he would wait for me. I made many calls as time passed to make sure he didn't want to cancel the appointment. We arrived at 5:30 p.m. His office was almost empty. But Dr. O'Day, the surgeon, Dr. Foshag, and the case manager were there.

He took us into his examination room. "I called Dr. Panera to find out some more about your situation. What you have is metastatic melanoma, which is incurable. The survival rate was six to twelve months among the patients over the past twenty years," Dr. O'Day said. "Even at early stages, favorable response rates to single-drug chemotherapy are at 10-20%."

"The CT scan I had in July before the hysterectomy showed cancer had not spread to the lymph nodes yet. Dr. Gray said it was stage I or II. When I had the operation in October, Dr. Eisner's report showed I was at stage III because cancer went to one lymph node." I basically just gave him a brief history of my condition.

"Yes, the metastatic melanoma is fast spreading and invasive. I recommend a six-month treatment program for you. This is a fifteen-year experimental bio-chemotherapy at our clinic, and this year is the fifteenth year."

"How does it work?" Lynton asked.

"It has four to six cycles of treatment. Each cycle includes five-day inpatient care using a combination of five chemo drugs, followed by twenty-one days of in-home care and rest. At the end of two to three cycles, there will be surgery to remove the shrunk tumors. After the surgery, there will be two or three more cycles of bio-chemo and possible additional surgery and conclude with radiation therapy."

The six months plan is impossible for me. I just went back to the classroom less than three months ago. I took two weeks off for the operation in October. There aren't too many sick leave days left. How can I keep my job? How can I take time off for the treatment with no income? Besides, Lynton just went back to school two months ago. I need my job.

All the thoughts flooded through my senses. *No, it's impossible! But how could I explain all this to the doctors?* "What other plans do you have?" I asked.

"We have two other plans. One uses single-drug chemotherapy and the other one uses a combination of two drugs. They have low survival rates. The third option is our experimental treatment, which is the bio-chemotherapy I mentioned. We administer the cocktail drugs together for five days in the hospital. Although the toxicity is considerably higher, preliminary studies show patients have a higher rate, about 40-50%, of responding well to the drug." Dr. O'Day explained.

"If I take this bio-chemo and have a satisfactory response, what are my chances of surviving?" I tried to calculate if it's worth doing it.

"We have been doing this for 15 years. There aren't enough statistics to show the survival rate yet. But, among the 40-50% favorable responses, 10-20% of patients have higher sustaining survival." Dr. O'Day elaborated.

"In other words, if I'm fortunate, I could be the 10-20% among the 40-50% of patients who survive if I respond well to the cocktail drugs." I tried to clarify. *The chances were still slim, but at least it was not zero.*

"This is our hope, and we want to see our patients have satisfactory responses and favorable outcomes."

"Do we need to decide right now?" Lynton asked.

"No, you can take your time to decide. Even if you decide to receive this chemo plan, you can stop at any point."

The surgeon, Dr. Foshag, came into the examination room halfway through our conversation.

"I know six months is a long time. It's worth taking six months out of your life to take care of yourself." Dr. Foshag detected the doubt on my face.

"I have a lot to think about." That was all I could say.

What he said struck my core. Taking care of myself has never been my priority. This information is enormously overwhelming. My head swells. My considerations come from all over the place. There is nowhere for me to get a grip at any point to start my thinking. Again, I'm not afraid to die. But I don't give up easily. I'll do my best to fight a good fight.

"I want to order the updated CT/PET scan and MRI for your brain and see if there were any changes since the last scan," Dr. Foshag said. "I'll monitor your inpatient stay at St. John's Health Center in Santa Monica."

"What is the worst damage caused by these toxic drugs? Will I recover from the damage?" I asked.

He didn't have to think before answering my questions. "The drugs might damage your liver or kidney and it is irreversible. But we don't know because it depends on how a patient responds to the drugs."

There seemed to be more unknown than known factors. I wasn't sure if I wanted to go with the aggressive treatment.

"We'll go home to talk about this. I'll let you know as soon as possible." I told the doctors.

"Here is the reading material. Take it home and think about that. Call me to let me know of your decision." Dr. O'Day responded with a gentle voice as the case manager handed me the article.

Lynton looked at me and said, "We'll take the paperwork home to read and talk it over with our family. We'll call you once we've decided."

"Sure, this is a major decision. We understand you need to think it over. We're here ready for you."

I paged Dr. Eisner at UCLA before leaving the doctor's office, but because of the holiday, he didn't return my call right away. I faxed him the information from The Angeles Clinic and asked for his advice.

Chapter 8

Crossroad

November 2008

After the appointment at The Angeles Clinic, we took surface streets to bypass the 405 freeway and get on the 105 freeway. It was very late by the time we got home. We had a quick dinner. Later in the evening, Mercy was coming downstairs as I was going upstairs to talk to her. We sat down on the top steps of the stairway.

"What did the doctors say?" She asked.

"The doctors said my cancer is incurable. But the clinic has an experimental treatment. They think it's more promising than the other two that are not effective."

"What's the experimental treatment?"

"This is the fifteenth year of their program. The doctors said there's a higher percentage of survival. It's a six-month full-time plan using five drugs." I showed her the paperwork from the doctor's office.

"This list explains each of the drugs and the short-term and long-term side effects. The short-term side effects are flu-like symptoms like diarrhea and vomiting. The long-term effects are nerve and liver damage. It seems like these drugs could kill my small body before they kill cancer," I said jokingly, but the images of the drugs invading my body frightened me.

"What are you going to do?" She asked.

"I don't know yet. Let's pray about that. I'll discuss this with Lynton's family because many of them work in the medical field."

~ ~ ~

On Thursday, we had Thanksgiving dinner at Lynton's brother Philip's home. They were aware of my diagnosis. I shared with them my meeting with Dr. O'Day and his recommendation.

"From my observation over the years, the single drug Interferon alone is not effective," Lynton's sister-in-law Barbara said. She was a case manager for discharge planning at Loma Linda Hospital. "Your new doctor's chemo plan is better."

It was helpful to have suggestions from the doctors, family, and friends, but ultimately, the decision was mine. Dr. Foshag ordered the updated CT/PET scan and MRI. I had to decide over the weekend if I wanted the treatment to start in January. It was the hardest decision I had ever made in my life.

Lynton and I continued to do research over the weekend. I must decide on Monday before cancer outruns me.

My mind came to a halt. *There are two roads in front of me. Which one should I choose? The road to the single chemo drug is ineffective. It may lead to a dead-end, eventually. The other road is unknown, with a slim chance of leading to healing.*

The Road Not Taken by Robert Frost came to my mind, especially the last few lines.

> *Two roads diverged in a wood, and I—*
> *I took the one less traveled by,*
> *And that has made all the difference.*

I gazed at the road of unknown. I sought affirmation.

What should I do? I'll die sooner if I don't choose the experimental treatment. The cancer is racing through my body at this moment. Has it spread beyond my abdomen yet? If I accept this bio-chemo plan, can my small body handle the harsh drugs? Even if I could handle the drugs, I would only have a 10-20% chance of survival. What should I do? I need a sign so clear that I have the conviction and courage to move forward.

The suggestions from the family were helpful, but I still needed a professional opinion.

Dr. Eisner was the chief and director of the oncology department, professor, and researcher at UCLA. He would be in the best position to make a recommendation for me. I had sent him the fax. I needed to hear from him.

The ultimate deciding factor would be the approval of the insurance. The Angeles Clinic and Research Institute was a private facility outside of my primary care system. It was expensive. I couldn't afford it if the insurance wouldn't cover the procedure.

If I get the green light from Dr. Eisner and the insurance, I will go ahead with the treatment.

Dr. Eisner called me on Monday afternoon after reading my fax. Before I said anything, he gave me a firm "yes" repeatedly. Then he said, "You should do it."

I said, "I should go with the bio-chemo plan?"

"Yes," he said, "you should do it because melanoma is a tricky thing. I just want to protect you."

Okay, with Dr. Eisner's firm recommendation and encouragement, the next step is getting the insurance approval.

~ ~ ~

In the meantime, I asked the church fellowship group to pray for my decision.

My health insurance was a Health Maintenance Organization (HMO). As suggested by the name, this type of insurance only provided the basic health maintenance needs. The doctors from St. Jude must submit a request to the insurance for authorization. I called The Angeles Clinic immediately to let them know of my tentative decision, depending on the insurance approval.

Dr. O'Day communicated with Dr. Panera at St. Jude. They jointly submitted the treatment request to the insurance for approval.

Chapter 9

Financial Relief

December 2008

Two weeks had gone by with no answer from St. Jude or The Angeles Clinic.

I should start my treatment right now!

No one knew if the insurance had approved the plan. No one followed up on the requests. I did my best to be the self-advocate to get the services. In a normal circumstance, I would just wait to hear from the insurance. This time, it was a race between life and death. The clock was ticking. I felt confused and frustrated.

My case was a complicated one. The Angeles Clinic was a private institute. It was not my primary medical group, so the doctors couldn't submit any request to the insurance directly. I needed lab work, EKG, CT/PET scan, and MRI of the brain before the chemotherapy. Each doctor's appointment and test needed a separate request to get authorization from the insurance. But nobody knew who should submit the requests to the insurance company.

After calling St. Jude customer services and complaining, the Case Management Supervisor called me. "I'm taking over your case. I'll make some calls to locate all the testing requests," she said. She was the same supervisor who arranged my appointment with Dr. Panera.

~ ~ ~

Ever since October, I discussed my cancer situation with some friends.

"Are you a member of the Catastrophic Leave Bank?" My friend Diann asked me. She was a teacher.

"No, I'm not. What is it about? What does it do?" I asked.

"You donate one sick leave day to the bank to become a member. After you exhausted your sick leave days at the district, you could withdraw the days from the bank, 20 days at a time to receive 50% of the pay. You could withdraw up to 100 days." Diann gave me the information.

"Thank you for the information. I'm not a member, but I'll talk to the Human Resources Office about it."

I was a school district administrator for ten years until six months ago. The administrative assistant at the Human Resources Office was always friendly to me. I needed to speak to her regarding taking six months off once I received the insurance approval.

"Hi Amy, I'll be in full-time treatment for my cancer for six months after the winter recess. Would you have your staff request a long-term substitute teacher for me?" I said, breaking the news to her.

"Sorry to hear that, Ms. Hurdle. Sure, I'll let Jane know and she will arrange it for you," she responded with a warm smile.

"Anyway, I would like to become a member of the Catastrophic Leave Bank."

"Teachers usually join the Bank at the beginning of the school year, but I'll set it up for you. Do you have one sick leave day to donate to the Bank?"

"I do. Do I need to sign any paper?"

"Yes, I'll get you the paper to sign. After you've exhausted your personal sick leave, you can take 20 days at a time from the Catastrophic Leave Bank up to 100 days. You just send me a letter every 20 workdays with the doctor's note."

"Thank you. It would help me get 50% pay for five months."

"Oh, now you're a teacher. Under the teachers' union contract, after you used up your personal sick leave days, you'll get 50% pay up to 100 additional sick days."

"I have sick leave days for one month. If the CLB pays 50% for 100 days and the union pays 50% for 100 days, with all three resources, they would cover me for the entire six months with full pay. This is very helpful. Thank you, Amy."

For a moment, the overwhelming joy made me forget about my cancer.

"You're welcome, Ms. Hurdle. I'm glad it works out for you."

I am in awe to find out the information about the CLB and the teachers' union. Lynton is in school until next summer. The provision of 100% pay for six months takes the heavy burden off my shoulder. Now, I just need the insurance approval.

Chapter 10

Test Preparation for Treatment

December 2008

Two weeks had gone by. There was no news from the insurance. Waiting was like seeing the time go by in slow motion and looking at the anxiety with a magnifying glass.

The students in my first/second-grade combination class did very well. It was gratifying to see students making steady progress. It took my mind off my distress most of the day.

The insurance approval finally came in the mail on December 18th. Phew! It was surreal. The huge mound of worries broke into pieces and dropped. I got the green light of Dr. Eisner's recommendation and the insurance approval. Those were the signs I asked for. I had passed the point of no return. I could only move forward.

Joy emailed me, "Being a cancer survivor myself, I have been praying this is the decision you would make. You want to look back and know you did all that you could do to beat this!"

"Thank you, Joy. I feel peaceful about my decision."

~ ~ ~

Diana from my primary care, St. Jude, called on the same day I received the letter from the insurance. "Ms. Hurdle, Gina at The Angeles Clinic and I will coordinate the treatment procedures. She and I will take care of you. She told me you need many tests and inpatient care at St. John's Health Center, their affiliated hospital. I'll submit the requests to your insurance. You're in no position to navigate the medical system. All you have to do now is to get well."

Did I hear it correctly? She and Gina will do everything for me? All I have to do is to get well?

"Thank you, Diana. Nobody knew what to do with my case for several months."

"You're welcome, Ms. Hurdle. Your first chemo at St. John is on January 7th."

"That's right, Gina told me on the phone."

"You'll receive copies of authorization letters from the insurance for all the tests I mentioned. You can call to make the appointments."

"Okay, thank you again."

~ ~ ~

After I received each authorization for my tests, I made the appointments to do them during the two weeks of winter recess. I got the appointment for CT/PET scan before Christmas.

A technologist from the imaging center called to review the preparation with me. He said, "Before the scan, stop taking medications for 48 hours, avoid exercising for 24 hours, follow a high protein diet for 12 to 24 hours, and not drink or eat anything, except water, for the last 6 hours." They sent me the paperwork prior to his call. So, I highlighted the things I needed to do as the technologist explained them to me on the phone.

On the day of the CT/PET scan, I drove to the Imaging Center, which was three miles from home. The technologist who called me greeted me.

In the waiting room, a technology assistant gave me a special dye called contrast media to drink before the scan. Contrast media can make the images from a CT scan easier to interpret. "Let me know when you finish the drink," he said.

After I finished, the technologist directed me to a small room and situated me in a tan leather chair. He then lowered it to put me in a reclining position.

"I'm giving you an injection of a radiotracer for the PET scan," he explained. "The radiotracer is to detect the higher levels of chemical activity, such as the metastatic melanoma in your body. It enters your veins through the IV. It will take 45 minutes for it to travel through your body. Go ahead and relax." After the injection, he dimmed the light and turned on a piece of soft music. I fell asleep.

The technologist came back after 45 minutes and took me to another room with a gigantic CT scan machine with a donut-shaped hole. I lay on a narrow sliding table.

"I'll strap your arms to the sides of your abdomen with Velcro so you can relax without worrying to keep your arms against your body," he said.

"I'll scan your abdomen and legs first, then the chest and the neck." He let me know exactly what he was going to do. "The table will slide slowly back and forth. Hold your body still without wiggling or coughing. I'll be in the control room and let you know when to breathe and when to hold your breath. The machine makes loud noises. Here are the earplugs to reduce the noise, but you still can hear me. Hold this button, press the button if you want to talk to me."

Fortunately, I was not claustrophobic to be in the tunnel. When he finished the procedure, he gave me a bottle of water.

The other two tests were MRI and EKG. I scheduled those for after Christmas. The MRI was for my brain to make sure cancer had not entered there. The EKG checked my heart rhythm to make sure I wouldn't die of cardiac arrest during the administration of chemo drugs.

The preparation kept me busy. At least I wasn't waiting and agonizing. It took my mind off worrying about my cancer.

My friend Rhonda sent me encouraging words. "It sounds like your persistence paid off. You'll get the tests done in time to start the treatment on the 7th of next month. I continue to pray for you every day–for the strength to get through these weeks and for your health ahead. We're with you each step of the way."

"Thank you, Rhonda! I can feel the strength of your prayer support."

~ ~ ~

Mercy scheduled to spend Christmas with us, but the airline canceled her flight because of the freezing rain and snow on the previous Sunday. The snow in Portland broke the last 100-year record.

"Mom, there's a one-stop flight coming to Ontario via Seattle, but I don't know if I could get on the connecting flight until I land in Seattle," she called me on the day of Christmas Eve.

"I want you to stay home and wait. If the snow stops, find out if there's a direct flight available in the next couple of days. It will be complicated if you couldn't get a connecting flight from Seattle. You'll have to find a place to stay overnight."

"Okay, Mom. I'll let you know."

The snow stopped the next day and Mercy got a direct flight arriving on the morning of Christmas day. There was no traffic on the drive to Ontario Airport to pick her up. Most of the people were where they wanted to be for Christmas.

It was so good to have Mercy with us for Christmas. We had our Christmas dinner at home. Her birthday is the day after Christmas. It warmed my heart to spend Christmas and her birthday together. Any amount of time with her is valuable.

~ ~ ~

School resumed on Monday after the winter recess. My hospital stay started on Wednesday. It worked out well because I could go to work on Monday. After school, I tidied up the classroom and prepared one week's worth of lesson plans. There would be a long-term substitute teacher for my class. She should be fine and acquainted with my class in a week. She would make lesson plans for the remaining six months.

Making a lesson plan for a substitute teacher was harder than teaching a class because I wrote detailed plans for them. After teaching for fourteen years, I could teach with simple lesson plans. I had the curriculum and resources at my fingertips and carried out the teaching according to the student's needs and made changes on the spot. The principals made sure the lesson plans were there. Being a teacher and an administrator for twenty-four years, I understood the importance of having lesson plans. There were a few times in my teaching days I needed a morning substitute teacher because of an emergency.

Okay, I put all the resource materials in an accessible area with labels. I also made a list of locations for other stuff. The substitute teacher could call me if he/she needs to find anything in my classroom. Goodbye, class, be good! I won't be back for the remainder of the school year.

Chapter 11

Preadmission for First Cycle of Treatment

January 2009

I checked my emails when I got home from school on Monday, January 5th, and opened the one from Mercy.

Hi Mom, I will pray for you a lot this week. Since you probably won't be able to talk to me on the phone, I'll call Lynton to see how you are doing. Also, I wanted to tell you what Will gave me for Christmas. I thought it might make you happy. It was a coupon for a date with him at the McMenamins Grand Lodge in Forest Grove. We both live with many housemates and constantly have people surrounding us. It will be nice to get away to be with each other. It seems like we have to go far away to be alone together. Talk to you soon, Mom.

I emailed her back.

Hi Mercy, nothing makes me happier than knowing that you have peace and assurance in your relationship with Will. Just seeing that you're happy makes me shed happy tears. I love you very much.

Mercy and Will graduated in 2007. They had been hanging out with each other since freshman. She told me about their dating when they were seniors. I secretly prayed that things would work out for them. Mercy lives in Portland by herself. I live in Southern California, 1,000 miles away from her. It would be a comfort knowing she was in a happy relationship and had someone to care for her.

She was my motivation to accept the treatment, hoping to live many more years to enjoy her. I wanted to see her getting married and having kids.

I checked some more emails and answered the phone calls from family and friends who extended their support.

~ ~ ~

My preadmission appointment was on Tuesday, January 6th. Annie, the RN at The Angeles Clinic and Research Institute reviewed and explained to me the treatment procedure.

She gave me a printed calendar marking the five days of hospitalization, and two and a half weeks of resting. I glanced at the calendar. There would be three days of Home Health Care by a nurse after the discharge. Then, I needed to have two and a half hours of IV, see a doctor or nurse at The Angeles Clinic once a week, and have blood tests twice a week.

The vigorous schedule was overwhelming. It gave me a headache trying to remember it. I had to rely on the printed calendar. No wonder I needed to take six months off for the full-time treatment. There was something going on every week.

"Please sign the consent form," Annie said.

~ ~ ~

Lynton had classes one day a week and an internship at a hospital for four days. My hospital stay was from Wednesday to Sunday. He could pick me up on Sunday. He traded one of the internship days so that he could take me to the follow-up appointments. I still needed rides on many days. He felt bad he couldn't take me to all the appointments.

It was inconvenient to get sick when he couldn't take care of me. But who could choose a convenient time to get sick? We just had to work it out and work through it.

Jolyn, from my church fellowship group, jumped in to coordinate the support for me. She sent out a request for people to sign up to give me rides. She also had people sign up to bring meals for me and Lynton twice a week. After she lined up the drivers and meal providers, she sent them reminders and also dropped me a note about my helpers of the week.

"When you bring meals to Miriam, please don't go in. She'll be in no shape to receive visitors." She sent out the message with a copy to let me know I shouldn't feel obligated to invite people in.

People rushed in to help me. Sharon emailed me before the sign-up sheet went out. Sharon had been praying for me from the beginning when I made my cancer known to the adult fellowship group.

Dear Miriam, if you need a ride to West LA on Monday, January 12th for the post-treatment appointment, Ken is available. He told me to tell you he is more than willing to drive you. He'll be there anytime you need him next Monday and any other time. As you know, he took early retirement this past summer. He is a good talker and listener in the car as well! Please let us know, Miriam. It would be our privilege to help you. Sharon.

I emailed her back and said my appointment was 8:00 a.m. and I had to leave the house at 6:30 a.m. She checked with Ken and got back to me right away. She said Ken was okay to pick me up at 6:30 a.m. Her warm email and willingness to help boost my spirit.

"Miriam, I can give you a ride on January 12th." Laura emailed me.

"Thank you, Laura. Lynton will take me on January 12th. Ken will give me a ride on the 22nd. Can you help me on the 27th?"

"Sure! I'll call you a couple of days before coming."

Having people to give me rides reduced Lynton's anxiety. These people were my extended family. I was grateful for their enthusiastic care and concern. The worries in my head had gradually dissipated.

I don't have to worry about the insurance. I don't have to worry about driving. I don't have to worry about cooking. Perhaps I can really focus on getting well.

Chapter 12

First Cycle of Bio-Chemotherapy

January 2009

The day I was waiting for finally came. It was my first inpatient treatment. On Wednesday, January 7th, my sister, Queenie, took me to St. John's Health Center in Santa Monica, 38 miles from home. After checking in at the admission desk, a nurse directed me to change into a gown. A patient transport specialist took me to a small operating room.

"I need to insert a Port-a-Cath beneath the skin under your left collarbone," the surgeon said. "It allows easy access for the nurse to give you medications by IV. It'll stay for the duration of your chemo treatment. I'll give you a local anesthetic, so you won't feel pain."

The procedure seemed to be quick and simple. A male patient transport specialist came and wheeled me to the hospital room. The nurse and the nurse assistant came to welcome me. They wrote their names and their extension numbers on the whiteboard. The nurse assistant took my vitals and told me she would do that for me several times a day.

Kathy, the nurse, was in her 50s with a round face, short hair, and a low voice. She reminded me of a colleague I worked with for the last ten years. She sat down on the left side of my bed and asked me questions while updating my patient information on the computer.

"I'll start the IV soon, but I'm going to insert a needle with a long tube into your Port-a-Cath first." She told me every little thing she did to keep me informed.

She checked the descriptions of four fluid bags, then hung them on the IV stand. *The large bag must be a saline solution, and the smaller bags must be the chemo drugs.* Before she inserted the cannulas into the end caps of the tube, she scrubbed each cannula gently with alcohol pads.

"Scrubbing it 100 times is the standard procedure for chemo patients," she told me with a smile. "I like to work with chemo patients. It has a lower nurse-patient ratio. We must have special training to be a chemo nurse."

"How many patients do you have?"

"I have four patients."

"I've been in the hospital multiple times. It's good you can spend more time with me."

"Chemo patients need more attention. You'll receive two drugs through IV and take three kinds orally. Each time you take oral medications, we'll tell you what they are," she said. "You'll experience side effects from the chemo drugs. I want to tell you what to do ahead of time. The drugs will cause diarrhea, vomiting, and flu-like symptoms such as shivers and fever. We call them chill and grill. When you feel the chills, press the button on this handle. We'll give you an injection to stop it right away."

"Okay. What are the other buttons on this remote?"

"The red button is to call the nurse, such as when you have chills or need any attention. Another button is to self-administer the pain medication by IV. There are buttons to turn the lights on and off or watch TV."

"Thank you."

~ ~ ~

I talked with Mercy on the phone.

"Hi Mercy, probably the drugs would make me too sick to talk to you in a couple of days. Wait for me to call you when I get home."

"Okay, Mom. I'll remember you every day."

I informed my family and friends the day before my first treatment. I didn't expect anyone to visit me at the hospital.

The first two days were almost normal. By the third day, the side effects hit me. Diarrhea and vomiting were horrible, so I ate very little, hoping if nothing went in, nothing would come out. I also had a foggy head, fatigue, and no voice.

The chills and fever started. It started with the shivering in my upper body and went down the legs. The teeth were in constant vibration, hitting up and down. I locked my teeth, tightened my jaw, stiffened my arm muscles, squeezed my elbows against the rib cage, and pressed my bent knees inward. As hard as I tried, there was no sign of stopping. It was not up to me to control it. I pressed the red button on the handle.

The nurse came in with a stack of warm blankets. She uncovered me. I curled up like a snail. She wrapped a warm blanket on my shoulder like a shawl and put two more on me, tugged them tight around my body, then added the previous blankets on top. She gave me a shot through the IV. In an instant, the warmth came upon me inside and out. I felt relaxed from head to toes.

"Don't wait too long next time. Call me as soon as the chill starts," the nurse said.

"Okay."

~ ~ ~

My body swelled with all the fluid going in and not being excreted in the same proportion. By the fourth and fifth days, I felt the burning under my skin like being in the blazing sun for hours. I could hardly walk with the heavy fluid in my body.

"You need to exercise every day. It helps with the fluid circulation," the nurse instructed me. "Holding the IV stand will give you some support when you walk."

"I'll try."

The IV stand looked six feet tall with five legs and rollers. It was my cane. Without that, I wouldn't be able to walk.

Lynton came on Saturday and stayed most of the day to keep me company. He brought his books to study. There was a bench/bed by the window where Lynton could rest during the day.

The discharge time was Sunday at 11:00 am. Lynton came to pick me up. But early in the morning, my potassium, magnesium, and electrolytes were very low. The attending doctor ordered replenishment through IV. It took seventeen hours before it finished. The doctor discharged me late in the evening.

The fluid put an additional 16 pounds in my body. It felt like lifting a 10-pound dumbbell on each foot when I walked. When I got home and looked at myself in the mirror with a brighter light, I looked like a balloon. It scared me to see a red plum face with dark purple around my eyes.

During my hospital stay, the nurse assistant gave me a sponge bath once, because I couldn't take a shower.

It took great effort to climb the stairs to get to the bedroom.

"I want to take a shower," I told Lynton. I spent all my energy climbing the stairs. There was no energy left to take another ten steps, so I crawled into the bathroom.

"Wait, you can't make the Port-a-Cath wet. It will cause infection. Let me cover it with plastic," he said.

He came back to the bathroom with a piece of plastic, clear packing tape, and scissors to seal the Port-a-Cath. He held the shower head while I sat in the bathtub to enjoy a warm shower. When the warm water poured onto my hair and my body, I closed my eyes and took every drop of water slowly. It felt like heaven.

Chapter 13

Home Health Care during Break

January 2009

There was a two-and-a-half-week break before the next cycle.

Even though we came home late on Sunday, January 11th, we still had to get up early in the morning on Monday. I had an 8:00 a.m. appointment at The Angeles Clinic. Lynton traded his shift with a colleague. He took me to the two and a half hours hydration appointment to flush out the toxicity. We left home at 6:30 a.m. to drive 38 miles through rush hour traffic.

The small IV room had one other patient undergoing the same therapy. The set-up was like an old-style Barber Shop with comfortable high-back chairs. A couple of seats were at the corners of the room for family members. The nurse hooked up the IV to my Port-a-Cath. I realized how convenient and painless it was without poking my arm or the back of my hand. The nurse also took blood for the lab work. Lynton brought enough books to study while waiting for me. I automatically grabbed a magazine, but it hurt my head trying to read.

When the hydration was over, we stopped by the store before getting home to pick up something I could eat. We bought some eggs, tofu, vegetables, and Jello. I wanted to go on a semi-liquid diet until my diarrhea and vomiting stopped.

In the afternoon, Lynton helped me pile up layers of blankets to make a sofa bed out of the couch in the living room. It was practical for me to rest downstairs throughout the day. Walking to our bedroom upstairs felt like carrying heavy weights around the ankles. I was glad Lynton stayed home on my first day of resting. I had never been that weak in my entire life. It felt strange.

Lynton was at work the rest of the week. A Home Health Care nurse came Tuesday through Thursday, from 10:00 a.m. to noon, to do the hydration through IV and check my vitals. By this time, my brain activity slowed down significantly. I fell asleep during the hydration.

My body sagged. I had about twenty percent energy. The long journey was ahead of me. I needed the physical strength to carry me through. It was crucial to move around the house frequently, though I dragged my feet slowly. My appetite was poor. My taste buds were dull. I cooked fresh vegetables, tofu, eggs, and chicken. I ate every two hours in salad plate portions. The vomiting continued, nothing seemed to stay in the stomach.

There were pills to help me urinate and reduce the body fluid. Frequent urination meant losing potassium. Potassium tablets helped replenish the loss. There were medications for pain, diarrhea, and vomiting. Lynton put the medications on the dining table. He made a list of medications and a schedule for me to take them. My brain was foggy. The list helped me to keep track.

By the second week, most of the excess fluid was excreted. I felt lighter. The chemo drugs suppressed my red and white blood cells significantly. My body didn't have enough blood to keep me warm. My skin felt like it was burning, but I was cold at the same time. I walked up and down the street a few times a day. The hooded heavy jacket, thick pants, and socks helped to keep the body heat from escaping. Nobody in the neighborhood said "hi" to this strange "bag lady."

I emailed an update to my family and friends about the side effects, the chills, fever, vomiting, diarrhea, burning under the skin, and delayed discharge. Many responses came.

January 13, 2009

> *Dear Miriam, it sounds awful! Call me for anything. Cleaning, food, whatever. I just want to*

repeat. CALL ME FOR ANYTHING! Will wait for your word. In the meantime, I continue to PRAY for you. Love to you both, Laura & Herb.

January 20, 2009

Hi Miriam, I came back from San Francisco last night, but have been thinking about you, praying for you to feel better. Your email sounds like you are miserable. I wonder if you could have a visitor. Could I drop in some afternoon? Let me know.

I'm hoping you can rest well and sleep soundly, that you can be better each day and feel more like yourself again. You are always so positive and hopeful. It was hard to see you going through so much. Love you, my friend. Rhonda.

I had a follow-up appointment on Thursday, January 22nd in the afternoon at The Angeles Clinic. Ken gave me a ride to the clinic. We didn't have a conversation in his van. *He knows my brain doesn't allow me to carry on a conversation.* When we arrived, there must have been twenty patients in the waiting room. A nurse saw me, so I didn't have to wait for too long. She checked my vitals and drew my blood for lab work.

~ ~ ~

People knew I was too weak to talk on the phone. They sent me cards and emailed me instead. I emailed them back when I had a little energy. They brought food for us on Tuesdays and Thursdays. Lynton was glad he didn't have to cook after driving 48 miles home from his internship in Loma Linda.

I sent out an update on January 24, 2009.

> *Dear family and friends, thank you for all the cards and emails with encouraging words. I feel like I'm floating peacefully on a soft but strong bed of prayer support. I'm resting with no struggle, no reasoning, no anxiety, no anticipation, no worries, no "plan," except hope, great hope to get well. I have no questions for God, except a grateful heart. Thank you for being in my life. Your prayers will carry me through to the end. Miriam.*

Mary replied to me on the same day.

> *Dear Miriam, I, too, am so glad for the news that you can praise God amid such trying circumstances. This encourages me to keep on upholding you even more. I have truly been keeping you before the Lord continually, hardly being able to imagine how sick you must have felt*

from the medications. To know that you are being upheld so powerfully is evidence of God's answers and I am filled with praise at His power! I see how God is using you to encourage us amid your greatest weakness! Keep on because of Him! Love, Mary.

Before I was ready, it was time for the next treatment cycle.

Chapter 14

Second Cycle of Bio-Chemotherapy

January 2009

During the break after my first cycle of chemo treatment, I emailed the update to my family and friends. Many of them responded to me. There was one email on January 19th from my family in Hong Kong. It was wonderful and surprising news from my brother-in-law, Patrick.

> *Dear family, today I received a call from the hospital in China that I can have a kidney transplant. I will have the operation tonight. It may last for 2+ hours. After that, I need to stay in the hospital for 3-4 weeks. I am confident that God will be with me. Please remember me in your prayer. Thank you for your support. Patrick.*

It was unbelievable. It was like yesterday when he had kidney failure. I didn't expect him to receive a kidney donation so soon.

In the summer of 2008, my husband Lynton, my daughter Mercy, her then-boyfriend (now husband) Will, and I wanted to attend my nephew's wedding in Hong Kong. That was the year when the Summer Olympics took place in China. The airfares going to Hong Kong from the US were higher than usual because people traveled to Beijing through Hong Kong. After searching, I found a Thailand tour via Hong Kong, and we could stay in Hong Kong for any length of time.

We went to Hong Kong and attended my nephew's beautiful wedding. Then we had a five-day tour in Thailand. When the tour was over, we came back to the US via Hong Kong. There was a two-hour layover.

While we were waiting at the Hong Kong airport, I called my sister Yolanda. To my surprise, there was worrisome news. While we were in Thailand, Patrick went to work on the train as usual. He got on the train but had a premonition that he should get off the train at the next station, and he did. As soon as he got off, he felt dizzy and fainted. Upon arriving in the Emergency Room, and being attended to by a doctor, he was diagnosed with kidney failure.

I felt sad about the news. Patrick and Yolanda had prepared for it because they had known about the possibility for quite some time. The doctor put Patrick on routine dialysis at the hospital as an outpatient service. Eventually, he learned to do it by himself at home. He was making a good adjustment.

He registered in the medical system in China to get a kidney donation. His blood type is O. He could only receive a kidney from people with blood type O, whereas individuals with any other blood type could accept a blood type O kidney. He has fewer chances to get the same blood type kidney. He was told that the waiting time was from two to ten years.

Patrick accepted the fact he had to wait for a long time to get a kidney donation. He quit his job to take care of himself. Yolanda was very supportive.

After six months of waiting, Patrick received a phone call from China; letting him know there was a kidney donation for him, and he had to go straight away for the transplant. Yolanda could not go with him without advanced notice of her government job. Patrick's sister went with him, taking the night train to China. Yolanda took time off to join Patrick the next day.

Yolanda kept me informed to let me know she stayed with Patrick for ten days while he went through testing, transplant surgery, and observation. Thankfully, the donor and receiver were a good match. Patrick's body didn't show any sign of rejection of the new kidney.

It was a miracle. The news gave me hope a miracle could happen to me as well.

Mary sent out this email to Joint Heirs, the church fellowship group, on January 25, 2009

> *Dear Joint Heirs, don't forget to continue to pray for Miriam. I believe she starts round two of her chemo on Wednesday. Pray that her body will be strengthened to withstand the onslaught of another round of chemo. Pray that the medication will hit its target and kill cancer. But also pray that her other organs will be protected from the strong medication. She is being so brave, and our prayers are helping. Thanks, Mary.*

My second cycle of inpatient care started on January 28, 2009. After I settled into my hospital room, I called Mercy.

"Hi Mercy, I'm in the hospital now. I just want to call you. I know I'll be very weak with no voice by the third day."

She was glad to hear from me. "I wish to be there with you, Mom. I want so much to visit you and just be in the hospital room with you."

I got teared up hearing her say that. "I know, Mercy. Knowing that you're thinking about me gives me strength. Lynton will keep you posted. I'll call you when I feel better next week."

The second cycle of treatment was worse because I hadn't totally recovered from the first cycle. I had different nurses and nurse assistants. Perhaps they thought I knew the routine, so they didn't spend extra time with me. It didn't bother me. I didn't have too much energy for conversation.

Lynton was working. Mercy was in Portland. My friends were 38 miles from the hospital.

I didn't expect to have any visitors. Who wanted to drive such a long distance to see me when I couldn't talk to them? When I worked in the school district office, I avoided going to conferences in West Los Angeles or Santa Monica. The traffic was horrible. I wouldn't blame anyone for not visiting me, even if I could converse with them.

I had a surprise visitor on the second day, January 29th. Hershey, a Labrador, and a staff member from Animal-Assisted Therapy came to see me. He was a well-trained, well-groomed, and gorgeous dog. He had a broad face, short hair, and an off-white color with a few patches of tan on his face. The staff pulled a chair close to my bed and had Hershey sit in it. He put his paw on my bed to let me pet him. I could reach him without sitting up. He didn't wiggle or do anything to startle me. It was a pleasant, short and sweet visit. It lasted for ten minutes. I was glad Hershey came before the drugs kicked in to make me sick.

A respiratory specialist came every day to give me breathing exercises. He asked me to sit on the edge of my bed and handed me an incentive spirometer. He asked me to hold the device in an upright position, place the mouthpiece in my mouth, and seal my lips tightly around it. The next thing was almost impossible for me to do. I had to breathe in slowly to make the yellow piston rise toward the top until reaching the blue outlined area. When I couldn't hold my breath, I let out the air to start again. I needed to do 10 successful times. He said the chemo drugs made me weak and the breathing exercise helped my lungs from collapsing. He asked me to do it every hour, but I probably did it a few times a day.

My vomiting, diarrhea, chills, and fever were the same as last time. My body got weaker and weaker when they happened. The frequent interruption of taking my oral medications and my vitals was the worst thing at the hospital. I didn't get too much sleep. Every little sound woke me up. I brought my prescribed sleeping aid, but the nurse said the hospital didn't allow taking medications from home. She got the doctor to prescribe Ambien for me. I told her I only wanted the regular strength, not the extra strength. I took the pill on the second night. When I woke up to see the meal tray by my bed, I thought it was breakfast. In fact, it was dinner. I slept for twenty hours. It was the only time I took Ambien.

I understood the chemo treatment was important, but I just wanted to go home.

Chapter 15

Reduced Treatment Cycles

February 2009

Lynton came to pick me up on Sunday, February 1st, the last day of my hospital stay. I had a fever. The attending doctor discharged me with medication to lower my temperature. My persistent fever of 102° F lasted for ten days. The medication didn't help a bit.

I feel there is no life left in me right now. I need miracles to carry me back to life.

I called Dr. O'Day. He asked me to see my family physician, Dr. Hutain, who was close to my home. Dr. Hutain ordered the lab work. The lab results showed my white blood cells were extremely low. That was the reason my body couldn't fight off the infection which caused the high fever. My red blood cells were also very low, which resulted in my fatigue. Dr. Hutain ordered antibiotics for the infection. He also ordered two units of blood for me to have transfused on February 11th to replenish my blood loss.

I had it done at St. Jude Medical Center. It took one and a half hours for the preparation and identification of my blood type. Two nurses came to the room with two units of Packed Red Cells (PRCs) with 350 ml in each. I realized afterward the human body has 10 units of whole blood. A healthy person can lose up to two units of blood without threatening their life. PRCs are units that have had the plasma expressed from a whole blood unit. Essentially, it has the same contribution to oxygen-carrying capacity as a whole blood unit but with less volume, since I had high retention of fluid from IV hydration.

The nurses read the labels on the clear plastic bags to each other to ensure they were identical. One nurse asked for my name and date of birth and checked the identity band on my wrist. I'm a universal donor with type O blood. But it meant that I could only receive type O blood. By the time the nurses were done with the preparation, I felt good about the process and felt relaxed for the six-hour transfusion.

The next day I felt a little energy coming back, so I went walking back and forth on the street again.

During the second cycle, like the first one, my body swelled with an additional 16 pounds of fluid at discharge.

"This is the handout for skincare," the discharge nurse gave me a stack of stapled paper. "It has a recommendation of body cream for extra dry skin. The lotion is too thin for your skin. You need to use cream. Here are some samples."

The accumulation of burning from the chemo drugs caused my skin to dry with blisters. When the swelling went down, the dead skin peeled off. The dry skin made me feel itchy, especially at night when nothing distracted my attention. I got medication for itching, but it didn't help. I soaked in a warm bath every night. When the dead skin got softened, I stroked it off. After I pat dry my body, I put one layer of lotion on every inch of the skin to let it absorb. Then I lavishly applied the cream and smoothened it with another layer of lotion. There were nights I was tired and tried to skip the bath. The itching was like hundreds of ant-bites that kept me awake. So, I got up to take a warm shower and followed the same regimen to apply the lotion and cream. The burning sensation caused another problem. It didn't let my legs touch each other when sleeping on my side. I needed to put a sheet in between to reduce the irritation.

"I picked up the new medications for you," Lynton reminded me. "They're for preventing you from a having blood clot or ulcer. There's also medication to ease the itching. I've added them to your list. Remember to drink plenty of water and juices."

"I know. When I drink too much, I get up every hour or two to go to the bathroom."

"Try to take naps during the days. The medications are hard on your kidney. You need to drink to flush out the toxin."

"Okay."

~ ~ ~

These were many emails I received from friends in February.

Miriam, so thankful for the information. It sounds like you are being so courageous through all these complications. Praying the fever will abate, and that you will find some rest and relief for a few days. God is good. I'm bringing dinner to you on Friday — so I'll call and see what sounds good to you and what is a good time to drop it by? God Bless & Keep You on these hard days, Rhonda.

Sharon consistently checked on me. *"I prayed for you Miriam, and God is walking through this with your hand in hand. God Bless you. Sharon."*

Miriam, I just read your e-mail about the prayer requests to Joint Heirs. I read them all and pray for you. I can't imagine what you are going through. I'm so very sorry that you have had to step onto this battlefield. I will continue to bring you before the Lord. May you always sense His presence with you - even in the darkest of times. I promise to keep praying. Love, Linda.

This email was from Lynton's sister, Janine.

Hi Miriam, Lynton was telling me how grueling it has been with this intense back-to-back treatment that barely gives you time to recover before the next round. Please remember that I have you in my prayers and am thinking about you often. Janine.

One day, I found a can of protein powder on my front porch, but there was no note. I texted Laura and asked if she left it there for me.

Miriam, yes, I left the protein powder at your door. When you are feeling better, we'll do something fun. Just try to build yourself up. Let me know if I can help. Laura.

I had lost ten pounds during the seven weeks of treatment! It sounded great, but nobody wanted my kind of diet plan though.

"Eat as much ice cream as you want," my friends said. "This is the time you can eat anything without worrying about gaining weight."

I took advantage of it and ate ice cream. I didn't have a sweet tooth, but it felt good not to worry about my weight.

I lost half of my hair, not quite bald yet. My sister, Queenie, bought me a wig. It was not custom-made. It would fit the oblong-shaped-head alien. I thanked her but returned it.

I chose not to shave my head. It was scary to wash my hair with chunks of hair falling into the bathtub. My hair was like black snowflakes falling all over the couches, the hallway, the kitchen, especially in the bathroom after each brushing. I loved my thick hair and wanted to hang on to every strand. At one point, Lynton said I looked like a punk!

~ ~ ~

There was a CT scan on Friday, February 13th to check my progress. The pre-admission for the third cycle and review of the CT scan was on Tuesday, February 17th at The Angeles Clinic.

On the day of the pre-admission, both Dr. O'Day and Dr. Foshag came to see me.

"You responded very well to the chemo drugs," Dr. O'Day said. "The CT scan showed the tumors have shrunk."

Dr. Foshag applied pressure on my abdomen and confirmed the tumors had shrunk.

"The original treatment plan was six cycles," Dr. O'Day continued. "You would have three cycles of chemo, a surgery to remove the shrunk tumors, and three more cycles. Instead of six cycles, you now only need four."

"That's right," Dr. Foshag agreed. "You had two cycles already. I'll do an operation for you to remove the tumors before your final two cycles of chemo."

When I heard the doctors' plan, even though I didn't have too much energy, I almost jumped up to thank them.

"Can I have some more time to rest before the surgery?" I pleaded. "There is no energy in me to handle the surgery."

"Yes, you can have a few more weeks to rest," Dr. O'Day agreed. "We can schedule the surgery in March, one month from now. By the end of the fourth cycle, you'll have a CT/PET scan and MRI of your brain for the assessment."

~ ~ ~

I emailed my family and friends to give them an update on the progress and good news. They've been worried about me. Many friends responded and cheered me on.

> *Dear Miriam, we are continuing to lift you up during this tenuous time. So glad to hear of the need for only two more cycles of bio-chemo. I pray our precious Heavenly Father envelops you with His love and comfort. We love you and care for you so very much. I've wanted to bring food over, but I've been so sick myself and I didn't want to compromise your situation. Love, Lynn.*

Some more emails from Lynton's sisters, Janine, and Vanessa, who received my update and emailed me.

Hi Miriam, I pray God continues to give you the strength that you need; and that you find encouragement and comfort from His powerful presence. Miriam, I really imagine seeing your Guardian Angel with you and watching closely over you. I'll send a prayer for you every night. Janine.

Dear Miriam, I hope today finds you feeling better and that your temperature has subsided. It is great news about the shrinking tumors. You seem to improve faster than the doctors had expected. Your strong faith in God cannot be underestimated, and it gives you the resilience to go through each day. Vanessa.

Emails and get-well cards continued to come. Some friends sent me cards periodically to let me know they remembered me. I hung up the cards on the window frame in the dining room. Whenever I felt weak and lonely, I read their emails and cards again and again. They were my constant reminder of people's sincere care and support. These people were my companions on this gruesome journey.

This is a miracle! I'm halfway done with my chemo treatment!

Chapter 16

Shrunk Tumors Surgery

March 2009

My surgery was on Thursday, March 19th, in the afternoon at St. John's Health Center. My sister, Queenie, took me there. She stayed with me until the patient transport specialist came to wheel me into the operating room.

I went into surgery at 2:30 p.m. I found out afterward my operation involved two procedures. The surgical team set up the room for the first procedure. When it was done, they changed the setup for the second one. It was 9:00 p.m. when Dr. Foshag finished the surgery. I was in my hospital room when I woke up at 10:30 p.m.

I couldn't go to sleep even though it was nighttime. I had slept for eight hours already.

"There's a button on this handle for self-administered pain medication," the nurse explained as she showed it to me. "Don't wait until you're in extreme pain to press the button. When it comes, press it."

She turned off the light for me and closed the door. I was awake all night.

The pain in my abdomen and my left leg came as no surprise. I did what she told me–press the button. I couldn't remember how many times I pressed the buttons. The sun came out. My head swirled like a whirlpool. *Did I give myself too much pain medication? I had no idea.*

On Friday morning, the nurse assistant came in with my breakfast. With great effort, I sat up and took a few bites. It didn't take too long for me to throw up everything.

The nurse assistant came back an hour later to take my vitals.

"Would you help me go to the bathroom?" I asked.

"Sure," she uncovered me. "Hang on to my arm."

She put one hand under my armpit and wrapped her other arm around my back to hold my other arm. As soon as I scooted to the edge of the bed, my body sank. I couldn't feel my left leg. Before I dropped all the way to the floor, she lifted me back to bed.

"Dr. Foshag put a nerve block on your left leg," she said as she examined the chart. "I'll be back with a bedpan for you to urinate."

I felt funny urinating in the bedpan. It felt like I wet the bed.

Dr. Foshag came to see me in the afternoon.

"I removed the cancerous inguinal lymph nodes in your left groin area. I got clear margins to make sure I took out all

85

the tumors," he said. "This is what it means to your leg. Inguinal nodes allow the fluid from your lower body to circulate to the upper body; then to the heart and circulate back to the lower body. Now your inguinal nodes are gone. The fluid from your left leg wants to go to the upper body, but it hits a dead end and turns back to the leg."

"My leg is swollen and painful. It feels like exploding."

"I know. The pain is from the surgery. I inserted a draining tube with a bottle from your left thigh to the lymph nodes area to catch the bottled-up fluid," he continued. "I want you to record the amount of drainage daily to determine when to remove the tube."

"What happens after you remove the tube? How long will the swelling last?"

"It may take six weeks to three months for the swelling to go down."

"But the fluid still can't circulate to my upper body. Will it be permanent?" I got worried.

"It's hard to say whether this will be permanent. I'll refer you to Lymphedema therapy. They can help you."

~ ~ ~

The attending doctor wouldn't discharge me until my leg woke up with some strength to walk. But my leg didn't cooperate all day on Friday.

On Saturday, the 22nd, my left leg was still numb but had some sensation. I stood up but couldn't bend the knee or put my body weight on the knee. The doctor said I could go home with a walker. I called Lynton to pick me up that afternoon.

~ ~ ~

I was miserable the first two days after I came home. The nerves from my left knee to the inner thigh and to the left side of the abdomen were numb. There were no knee muscles to support my body when I used the stairs. I used the right leg and dragged the left leg up and down the stairs. When getting up from a chair, I used my hands to push the seat to prop up my body.

I called Dr. Foshag on March 25th. He was in surgery, so I left a message. The receptionist said he would call me when he finished the surgery. He returned my call late in the afternoon. I told him about my numbness and swelling.

"It might take a couple of weeks for the numbness to go away. As far as the swelling, you need to lie flat and elevate your legs above your heart to reduce the swelling. You also need to get up and move around."

"I'll try."

"How much is the drainage?"

"It has been about 140 ml each day."

"Continue to record the amount of drainage. I'll remove the tube when it gets to be less than 40 ml for three consecutive days."

"Okay."

~ ~ ~

Lynton took a week off from his school and internship to help me get around. I was clumsy getting up and down. It was helpful when he handed me the medication, water, or anything I needed.

I went to see a lymphedema therapist. She measured and compared my two legs from the ankles to the top of the thigh to set a baseline. She showed me how to massage upward from the knee to my upper body with a single stroke at a time.

"There're many ways to treat lymphedema," Fran showed me a brochure. "In extreme cases, we use strapping besides massage and exercise to reduce the swelling. In your situation, you're dealing with missing lymph nodes. You'll massage to reduce the swelling. But you'll also train the fluid to take a detour to circulate to the upper body."

"I can't bend down to massage from my knee to the thigh," I told her.

"That's right. For now, you can lie on the couch and try to lift your leg to massage. Don't rub it hard, just gently caress your skin upward."

I emailed my family and friends to update them about my surgery, the intolerable pain, and the swelling leg.

"Miriam, we will be praying for you and your leg! BE CAREFUL WITH THOSE STAIRS! As I said before, you are amazing! Christy and Mark." Christy kept up with my condition. I was thankful she gave me a ride once to The Angeles Clinic. Her daughter Janelle was a student at UCLA. She took orange juice to Janelle every week. After dropping me off at the clinic, she visited Janelle and came back to pick me up.

"Miriam, we will definitely pray for your leg to return to full function. I will share it with Bible Study tonight. Sally." Sally also gave me a ride to the clinic for my follow-up appointment.

Sharon brought me meals, and her husband, Ken, gave me rides. She emailed me on multiple occasions.

> *Miriam, you are so blessed. The numbness sounds like a temporary thing. I hope today the feeling is coming back. I don't like to be sick to my stomach, so I feel bad for you about that. But again, that is temporary. When you feel up to it, let us know when you need anything. As I remember, Lynton was going to be home the first week with you. If you need meals or just want some company, send us an email. Jolynn coordinates your drivers, so I*

will tell her Ken is available. I can't tell you how wonderful it is to hear this is behind you. We'll keep on praying that the pain subsides quickly and that the days do not seem long! Sharon.

My follow-up with Dr. Foshag was on March 31st. He would tell me more about the surgery result. Dr. O'Day would be there to let me know about the rest of my treatment.

I know the pain won't go away just yet. God, please give me the strength to tolerate it until it subsides. I read a message that faith is a process. If pain is a process to develop stronger faith, I'm thankful for the process. I have no complaint and am grateful that I'm still alive.

Chapter 17

Shepherd's Pie

March/April 2009

If someone told me the extent of the side effects the chemo caused, would I still want to go through the treatment? I don't know.

Dr. Foshag gave me six weeks to rest before the third cycle of chemo. During those six weeks, my only job was to get strong enough for the subsequent treatment.

He asked me to record the drainage collected by the two bottles. During the two weeks after the surgery, one bottle inserted into the incision got less and less fluid. The one with a rubber tube inserted from my left thigh to the lymph node area had 135 ml of fluid every day. It seemed like the fluid just didn't circulate to my upper body. The only outlet was through the drainage. I lay on the couch and elevated my legs above my heart as the doctor instructed. It helped to reduce the ballooning of the leg. There was no sensation in my left leg from the thigh to the ankle. I wouldn't feel any pain if I pierced it with a knife. Regardless, I got up every hour to move around the house, even though I didn't feel the difference it made.

On Tuesday, March 31st, I went to Dr. Foshag for my follow-up appointment.

"The CT scan right after the surgery showed clear. I got all the tumors. The incision looks good. I'll remove the staples," he said. "The stitches in the deeper tissues will dissolve by themselves."

I showed him my recording of the drainage. "One bottle is getting less and less fluid, but the other one has 135 ml every day for two weeks."

"I'll remove the first drainage but keep the other one for two more weeks. Continue to record the fluid amount."

"What if it'll be the same in two weeks?"

"Try your best to massage the leg. I'll prescribe a compression stocking for you. Here's the company's business card. Call them to make an appointment for the measurement."

"The lymphedema therapist, Fran, mentioned the compression stocking."

"Continue to see her. She'll give you the ongoing therapy. I'll see you in two weeks."

"Okay. I'll make an appointment to come back."

~ ~ ~

Two weeks went by. The drainage was about 60 ml each day. I went to see Dr. Foshag. He removed the second bottle even though it didn't decrease to 35ml as he wanted. He asked me to work with Fran, continue to massage my leg, and wear the compression stocking.

~ ~ ~

The chemo drugs wiped out a wide range of cells indiscriminately without focusing on the cancerous cells. They burned all the cells in me, good and bad. I was down to skin and bone. The burning that dried up my skin got worse. I diligently soaked in the hot bath for an hour each night. There were a few nights I couldn't get enough hot water from the faucet. It must be something wrong with the hot water heater. Lynton boiled the water on the stove and carried pots of hot water upstairs to fill the bathtub. I will never forget that.

I had a terrible time falling asleep. Rather than agonizing, tossing, and turning in bed, I got up quietly without waking Lynton. Following a few yoga movements for the lower body, I stretched my legs, doing lunges, squats, and forward folds. I massaged the fluid from the legs to my upper body. After an hour or longer of stretching, I massaged my head in bed and listened to music from my headphones to relax. It was a lot of work to get some sleep. Lynton kept quiet when he woke up in the morning. It was about nine or ten o'clock when I woke up.

During this time, the world was thousands of miles away from me. The pain, discomfort, and weakness were ever-present. Many cards and emails continued to come. Several friends created handmade cards with uplifting messages for me. They didn't just send me the cards once. They came periodically with lovely designs.

One gentleman sent me an email, "I continue to pray for you. Hang in there and know others support you in prayer; some you may not know, but care very much."

Our friend Dr. John Sailhamer was a Bible scholar and professor, fluent in Hebrew and Greek. He wrote many books and Bible commentaries. He was diagnosed with Alzheimer's disease at the same time I was diagnosed with cancer. It was during the early stages of his disease that I began my chemo treatment. While he was receiving treatment, he translated Psalm 1 in the Bible directly from Hebrew and handwrote it for me. His kindness touched me tremendously. I read his translation and meditated on one keyword a day. It gave me the comfort of knowing God cares about me.

At the last appointment, Dr. O'Day said I needed to gain about six pounds to better handle the next chemo treatment. I had six weeks to achieve the goal. With this mindset, I ate whatever and whenever my stomach allowed. Several neighbors, Doris, Gina, and Debbie had been our friends for over twenty years. They invited us over for dinners. Doris invited us almost every weekend. Her son Randy, Lynton's best friend, barbecued steaks. Doris said, "Miriam, eat. The meat will help to replenish your blood."

I did. I ate the biggest piece of steak on the platter. She was so pleased I could eat. She told everybody, including her dental hygiene patients I ate the biggest piece of steak. What was for dessert? Fresh strawberries with vanilla ice cream. Without the chemo drugs' interruption, my stomach kept all the food down.

Lynton drove 48 miles each way, five days a week, for his classes and internship. He didn't have too much time to do cooking every day. He made vast pots of *shepherd's pie* on the weekends and froze it into dinner portions. We had *shepherd's pie* for every meal for several months straight.

My daughter Mercy was glad I only had two more cycles of treatment. She called me in April prior to my third cycle.

"Mom, sorry I can't come to see you when you're in the hospital. I want to come in the summer."

"Don't worry. I know you're new to your job. You can't take time off. When do you want to come?"

"I want to do something with you to celebrate your health. When will you finish your treatment?"

"I should finish all the chemo by the middle of June."

"I can come in July and stay for a week. I hope you'll feel good enough for us to do something."

"I'm sure we can do that. I'll start thinking about what we can do and let you know."

"Sounds good, Mom. We'll talk some more soon."

"Okay, Mercy. Call me if I don't call you first."

"Love you, Mom."

"Love you, Mercy."

I saw Mercy in Christmas 2008. It was exciting to know I'd see her at the end of my treatment. She called me almost every day, but it was nothing like seeing her in person. There were many things I wanted to talk about with her. I wanted to know more about her job, her life, and her relationship with Will. I wished it was July already. I might not have normal strength yet, but it would be wonderful to see her soon and do things with her.

Chapter 18

Last Two Cycles of Bio-Chemotherapy

May/June 2009

The third cycle of chemo started on May 6th. The inpatient care routine was the same as the previous ones. At discharge, it only gave me additional 12 pounds of fluid instead of 16. I came home on the 10th. The swelling of my left leg got a double hit from the chemo and the surgery. The pressure of the swelling was intolerable.

I visited the lymphedema specialist, Fran, in her office. She measured the circumference of both legs in three-inch increments from my ankle to my thigh to check the progress.

"Your body won't regenerate the lymph nodes after being removed," she said. "The therapy isn't for healing but for educational purposes. The more you understand, the better you can cope with the situation."

During my first visit, she mentioned in some of her patients' extreme cases, they used elastic to strap around the affected areas. Even though she didn't ask me to do strapping, I wanted to try anyway. I bought two rolls of elastic sports wrap with clips to wrap my entire left leg, then lay on the couch and elevated my legs. It gave me temporary control of the build-up of fluid. I left the sports wraps on my leg until bedtime. It seemed to ease the burning sensation and it took me less time to fall asleep.

~ ~ ~

Mercy's email brought me some good news. She said that Will and she had talked about getting married and having a family. As soon as I read the email, I called her to ask for more details.

"Hi Mercy, I'm excited about your good news. I know you're coming in July, but I want to see you and Will at the end of June, a couple of weeks after my last treatment."

"I like that, Mom. I have a full house of housemates, though."

"Don't worry. We'll stay in the same hotel and rent a car. We'll be there just for the weekend. I still have a couple of procedures for my treatment when I return home."

"That's great. We'll talk some more about that, Mom."

"See you soon, Mercy."

~ ~ ~

Mercy's good news boosted my spirit. She hadn't seen me for five and a half months. I lost half of my hair during the treatment. It might shock her to see my look when we visit her in June. So, I took selfies of the front and side views of my head and hair during the last two months. I emailed them to her the next day.

I called her in the evening.

"Hi Mercy, I sent you an email. Have you received it? I lost a lot of hair, so I sent you my selfies. What do you think about my look?"

"You look just fine, Mom. Thanks for the photos."

"My skin looks funny because it peels off in patches. Some spots are darker, and some are lighter. I wish my skin would shed like snakeskin and come off nice and neat in one piece."

"Don't worry, Mom. You're healing nicely."

"I know, Mercy. My skin has peeled off many times. At least I'm getting brand new skin faster than normal."

"I admire your strength, Mom. You're a good example to me."

"Thank you for saying that. Mercy."

"You're welcome, Mom. See you soon."

My heart was warm when Mercy said I was a good example to her. It's worth all my physical suffering. This is any mother's dream to be an example to her daughters.

~ ~ ~

The break between the third and fourth cycles of inpatient treatment seemed to go by faster than the previous ones. I started my last cycle of hospital stay on Wednesday, June 3rd. Strangely, I felt okay when I checked in to the hospital and settled in my hospital room. A couple of hours later, I had a fever of 103°. The doctor put all the chemo drugs on hold and suspended the IV hydration. He ordered a chest X-ray, ultrasound for my heart, and blood culture, to make sure I didn't have an infection anywhere in my body.

"If the infection causes your fever, the chemo drugs will further weaken your immune system," the doctor explained to me. "I have to be cautious and do all the testing because the infection is dangerous when you can't fight it off."

The doctor waited until he got the blood culture result on Thursday the 4th before he resumed giving me all the medications. After five days of chemotherapy, he kept me in the hospital for one more day to do the observation. I was on IV antibiotics during the seven days of inpatient stay plus five days of oral antibiotics at home. He ordered a repeat of the blood culture at the end of the antibiotics.

A few days later, a nurse called to let me know the blood culture was negative. The Home Health Care nurse monitored my body temperature for three days during her visits.

The accumulation of the swelling in my left leg was horrible. I waited as long as I could before calling the doctor. It wasn't any better ten days after the discharge. So, I called. He was a little reluctant to prescribe the water pills to me, but he did it to help my body get rid of excess fluid. As he previously did, he also prescribed potassium to replenish the loss. As the excess fluid left my body, I was down to 114 pounds.

I was now able to walk up and down the street. After a couple of weeks, I walked around Laguna Lake with Lynton. Laguna Lake is about 0.7 miles south of our home. There are 0.77 miles around the kidney shape lake. Lynton used to run to the lake from home and run around it two or three times. He hadn't done that regularly this year because of his school and internship. He was happy to drive me there and walk with me. The sun was not too hot in the May afternoons. I walked slowly and stopped often to sit on the benches to watch the ducks. Egyptian Geese, with dark shades around their eyes, were new and extraordinary arrivals. There were many people, young and old, fishing with simple or complex rods and reels. It was refreshing to see mothers walking with their babies in strollers. Others were riding their bicycles or horses. The shimmering waters reflected the setting sun.

I felt positive, mentally and emotionally, knowing my cancer journey was approaching the end. It was surreal that I had come this far. My mind was alert. I spent more time on the computer writing my journal, reflecting on the meaning and value of life. The following poem came to me.

The Sun Welcomes Me

Journey through high and low
    amid worrisome melanoma cancer.
The sense of mortality heightened, with
    no assumption of
    survival chances.
My prayer was to ask for
    the mercy of the Maker
    granting me one more moment to live.
Every new morning was a precious gift.
Cloudy or sunny, the sky might be,
    rain or wind, caused the bones to chill in me.
Trotting on the street,
    even when having no energy
    to pick up my feet.
Hoping to keep up
    my physical strength

to sustain through six months of

harsh chemotherapy.

What a profound gratefulness I had as

treatment fading at the end

When the sun pierced through

the clouds to

welcome me.

Chapter 19

My Daughter Mercy's Visit

July 2009

There were two more procedures to complete my cancer treatment. One was the surgery to remove the last tumors. The other one was radiation.

After the last cycle of chemo, I had a follow-up meeting appointment on June 16th. Dr. O'Day ordered MRI for my brain and a CT/PET scan for my pelvic area. I was at his office on June 23rd to review the results. Both Dr. O'Day and Dr. Foshag were there to see me.

"The MRI and CT scan results are negative. You had a marvelous response to the chemo. That cancer is dead," Dr. O'Day said with a grin. He looked like it was his victory to beat my cancer.

The doctors seem to be ready to celebrate their success. I'm glad I made it alive instead of becoming a statistic and a casualty of their experiment.

"You had surgery to remove the tumors in the deeper inguinal nodes in the left groin. There's still one dead tumor in the initial cancerous superficial lymph node on the right." Dr. O'Day continued.

"I'll schedule the last operation to remove that tumor, so you'll have peace of mind," Dr. Foshag reminded me the job was not complete yet. "It'll be an outpatient procedure, but you'll stay in the recovery room overnight for observation after the surgery."

"When do you want to do that?" I wished there wasn't any more surgery because Mercy planned to see me in July.

"Early July is good. It gives you four weeks to rest from your last chemo."

Dr. O'Day looked at the chart in his hands. "I'll also order the radiation for you to do later in July. After your final surgery at St. John, you can schedule to have the radiation done at St. Jude."

~ ~ ~

The surgery was on July 3rd at St. John's Health Center. A draining tube was inserted from my right thigh to the superficial lymph node. Dr. Foshag wanted to leave it in for three weeks. He asked me to record the daily amount of drained fluid the same way I did previously.

Right after the surgery, I met with the radiation doctor on July 7th. After reviewing the order, she explained the procedure to me.

"Your radiation is five days a week for four weeks in the pelvic area. You'll come in at the same time every day. If you miss any day, you'll make it up on the other day during the same week."

"Will I feel any pain?" I asked.

"No, you won't feel pain. But there are possible side effects and damage to your body. You'll have permanently scarred tissues. Radiation in the pelvic area might change your bowel habit, cause bladder inflammation and pain in your abdomen, and feeling like you need to pass urine more often. Sometimes, it can cause fine cracks in the pelvic bones."

"It sounds serious. I would like to talk to Dr. O'Day about that."

"In the meantime, let's go to the radiation room. I'll align you with the radiation machine and mark your body with three tattoos, so each radiation will be done in a precise position."

~ ~ ~

After I got home from the meeting, I told Lynton what the radiation doctor said about the side effects and potential damage. He wanted to go with me to talk to Dr. O'Day.

I had a post-op appointment with Dr. Foshag on the following day. Dr. O'Day was there as well. Dr. Foshag reviewed the surgery results with us. He said he removed one large dead tumor plus fifteen small ones.

Lynton discussed the side effects situation with the doctors and voiced his concern about the potential damage. Dr. O'Day decided the damage outweighed the benefit. He adjusted the order to once a week for four weeks. The radiation concluded my year-long cancer treatment.

~ ~ ~

I received Mercy's itinerary of her visit from July 22nd to the 29th. I looked forward to this moment since January 7th, the first day of my first inpatient chemo treatment. I gazed through the tunnel, holding on to the fainted dim light at the end, and pressed forward. The light of seeing Mercy and spending time with her gave me strength and motivated me to fight for my life. Her voice on the phone was soothing, like a balm to my fragile body. Knowing I would see her in person soon warmed my heart and put a smile on my face.

I called her to get an idea of what she would like to do.

"Mom, I remember having so much fun going to Candlelight Pavilion for dinner shows. Do you think you can get tickets?"

"I'm sure they still have tickets. I'll call as soon as we're done talking on the phone. We started going when you were six years old. We purchased the season tickets for several years."

"I know. The Christmas show was my favorite."

"I remember that. During the last song, Santa invited all the children to go on the stage and gather around Mr. and Mrs. Santa. The youngest one could sit on Santa's lap. We took you to the front of the stage and Santa's assistant helped you to get onto the stage. The kids younger than you sat on Santa's lap."

"One time, the actor and actress came to our box."

"It was a surprise. During the intermission, the actors and actresses went around to visit the children. I was glad we were still there when they came. One actor held you in his arms to let us take some photos."

"I have great memories of going to the shows. I hope you can get tickets."

"I'll let you know as soon as I find out. What else would you like to do?"

"It takes about a two-hour drive to go to the beach from Portland. Maybe we can go to the beach."

"It sounds good. Which beach do you want to go to? Huntington Beach, Newport Beach, or Laguna Beach."

"What do you think? Which beach is easier for your walk?"

"I think Laguna Beach is pretty this time of the year."

"I like that. Oh, can we go to Disneyland? I know I'm not a kid anymore, but I had so much fun there."

"No, Mercy, Disneyland isn't just for kids. There are activities adults enjoy."

"Oh, good. We have three major things going. I hope you'll have the energy to do them. We'll play by ear the rest of the time."

"I'm happy we got some meaningful activities planned. I look forward to them."

"Me too, Mom."

I called Candlelight Pavilion right away and secured three rear-booth seats. I asked Lynton to purchase the Disneyland admission tickets online. Lynton completed his classes and internship. He was free in July while looking for a job so he could go with us.

~ ~ ~

Mercy arrived safely on July 22nd. We did something locally on the 22nd and 23rd.

We went to Laguna Beach on Friday the 24th and Lynton drove us there. It is 34 miles from our home. It's known for its many art galleries, caves, tide pools, ocean side bluffs, and, of course, sandy beach, all within city limits. The beach is also a popular surf spot because of its high tide.

We left in the late morning and arrived in time for lunch. There were several spots we used to park our car. On this day, we parked several blocks from the ocean front and walked to the beach. It was sunny and warm, but I wore a long sleeve top and a hat to protect my skin.

"Do you want to have lunch before walking on the beach?" Lynton asked.

"Sounds good. I'm hungry. What would you like to eat, Mercy?"

"Salad is good."

"The restaurant at the beginning of the boardwalk has fish platters, fish & chips, and several kinds of salad," Lynton remembered.

"I like the fish & chips I had there from our last trip. Do you eat fish, Mercy?"

"No, veggie salad is fine with me."

"Let's go then." Lynton led the way.

After lunch, we didn't walk on the sand as my feet couldn't pick up the pace very well. We followed the mile-long boardwalk leading to the paths and gardens of the oceanfront Heisler Park. Mercy made sure I was not tired from walking and suggested I sit and rest often. The tide was 10 feet high, as I found out afterward. I took several photos of rolling waves and water crashing the rocks.

Laguna Beach

Laguna Beach

Laguna Beach

We went to see a show at the Candlelight Pavilion on Saurday the 25th. I forgot what the show was about. It was enough for me to be with Mercy at the theater, which meant so much to us when she grew up.

Candlelight Pavilion

~ ~ ~

On Wednesday 28th, the day before Mercy returned to Portland, we went to Disneyland. Disneyland is eight miles south of our home. Our neighbor, Lynton's best friend, Randy, went with us.

Lynton and Randy went to the attractions and got the tickets at the designated time to return without waiting. I went with them on some rides but waited and watched when they went on some high adrenaline rides.

Lynton, Randy, and Mercy, Disneyland

Disneyland with Minnie and Micky

I appreciated Mercy spending eight days with me at the end of my treatment to celebrate the return of my health. This was the most meaningful week of my cancer journey.

Chapter 20

Life After Cancer

2009 to 2022

I only had one month to rest before going back to work. Was I ready to go back to it? No. Did I have the energy to work for another year? No. Why did I do that? By 2009, I had put in 24 years in the school district. The State Teacher Retirement System (STRS) calculates the retirement benefit based on the number of years served. If I had stopped at 24 years, my retirement income would be based on the average of the highest salaries for three consecutive years. Comparatively, if I had 25 years, it would be based on one highest salary year. For this reason, I went back to work for one more year. Besides, as I mentioned at the beginning of this book, I purchased five years of service credit intending to have 30 years for my retirement. I needed to make the payments for one more year.

Fortunately, my assignment was teaching 3rd grade. It turned out to be my favorite grade. The students had learned how to read from kindergarten to third grade. From the fourth grade and up, they read to learn the different subject matters.

My third-grade students were smart and worked hard. Most of them didn't cause any major problems in the classroom. One student got in trouble with another third grader and made her cry. I asked the girl what happened. She said, "Jose said I was pregnant." I tried hard not to laugh. When the students came back to the classrooms after recess, I talked with both students in the hallway and had Jose apologize to the girl.

Problems such as this weren't physically demanding. I was grateful because I was not in a good shape to carry out my daily duty. My immune system had a very low ability to fight germs. During that year, whenever one co-worker was sick, I got sick. Whenever a student in my class was sick, I got sick. I had a severe cold three times. My sick leave days were diminishing. Instead of taking a whole day off, I left work two hours early to go to the doctor. Normally, I needed a substitute teacher for those two hours, or if another teacher took my class for two hours, the district paid her for two hours. The 3rd-grade teacher next door also planned on retiring. She helped me out by taking my class without doing the paperwork, so she didn't get paid. As a result, the district didn't subtract two hours of sick leave from me.

All the teachers were very helpful to me. Toward the end of the school year, one teacher coordinated some activities to take photos of my class and interviewed some of my students about what they did in my class and what they thought of me.

She collected the information and made a shadow box to present to me at my retirement party in June 2010.

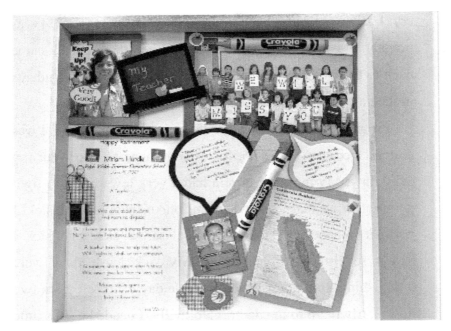

During the first year of cancer remission, I had no energy to do anything except get through my teaching every day. One day, I went to a store to get a hummingbird feeder. The pet section was in the back of the store in the far-right corner. When I checked out at the cashier in the front part of the store, I changed my mind about the color. I asked the cashier to have someone get me another color. She wouldn't do that for me.

I looked at the corner of the pet section diagonally from where I was standing. My body shrank to the bottom of an enormous mountain in front of me. I only had enough energy to go home. So, I left the hummingbird feeder with the cashier. Getting another color for the feeder would be another task for another day!

As far as the follow-up on my cancer, The Angeles Clinic set up a vigorous "surveillance" program for me. For the first year, I had lab work and a doctor's appointment every three months, and CT/PET scans every six months. From the second to the fifth year, the doctor's visits were every six months which included lab work. The CT/PET scan was done once a year. From the sixth year on, the doctor's visit, lab work, and CT/PET scans were done yearly. After ten years of negative results in the scans, the insurance didn't approve of having it done anymore. I continue to see the doctors and have the lab work done once a year.

The chemo treatment left permanent nerve damage to both of my legs. I had nerve tests by a neurologist twice. The results showed the roots of the nerves are not dead, only the superficial nerves are damaged. It is enough to cause tingling and numbness on my legs and keep me up at night. The damage is irreversible. My current doctor, Dr. Hamid at The Angeles Clinic, prescribed medication to calm my nerve. I take it at night to help me sleep.

The swelling of my legs from the removal of the lymph nodes is permanent. I wear a compression stocking on my left leg daily. Sometimes I get lazy and don't wear it. The pressure from the ballooning of my leg warns me not to do it again.

With new limitations came a new normal. My new normal seemed to focus more on myself and less on work, hence, less productivity. At first, it bothered me. I had plenty of time to reflect on the meaning of life.

Does a good life mean having a large volume of productivity? Does it mean it's good when it has a more successful outcome? Who remembers the hard work I did last year, two years ago, or ten years ago? I have a daughter and two granddaughters. My love for them is equal. I love their being, not their doing. Every being is valuable even if they can't produce anything.

I had lymphedema therapy and physical therapy for two years. My new routine was to elevate my legs above the heart level daily. I piled up the pillows on both sides of the loveseat and lay on it in a V shape with my head on one end and my legs on the other end.

I took yoga twice a week for two years. When two of my favorite instructors left, I lost interest in the subsequent instructors. I have been going to the gym to walk on the treadmill, use the weight-resistant machine and do swimming. My floor exercise involves laying on the floor, and stretching all parts of my body, especially my legs, to facilitate circulation.

Our family has grown in numbers and in blessings. Mercy and Will went camping on the July 4, 2010, weekend, and Will proposed to Mercy. My friend hosted a bridal shower for her. She and her maid of honor came. My friend was thrilled to have over 40 ladies come to the party. I was excited to be involved in Mercy's wedding planning. I flew up to Portland, Oregon, for a couple of days to help her pick out her wedding gown. I wanted to sing the song, "The Lord's Prayer" at her wedding. The treatment was hard on my voice, but I kept practicing. Just in case I couldn't hit the Bb note, I invited two of my sisters to sing with me. I sent the soundtracks to them to practice separately. The beautiful wedding was on May 28, 2011. The bride and groom couldn't contain their radiant smiles. And I hit the Bb note singing at their wedding.

Beautiful bride and groom, and family, May 2011

Happy bride and mother of the bride

Miriam's sisters Queenie (left) and Yolanda (right)

Mercy and Will, honeymoon at Marigot Bay, Lucia

Mercy and Will are blessed with two beautiful and intelligent daughters. Autumn was born on September 28, 2017, and Nora was born on March 22, 2020. Lynton and I visit them in Portland, Oregon, every six weeks. We love to watch the kids and encourage Mercy and Will to go on dates.

Welcome home, Autumn, October 2017

Welcome home, Nora, March 2020

Grandpa reading to Autumn and Nora, June 2022

Christmas, 2011

Sister Love, 2022

Mother's Day, 2021

Family walk, biking, and skateboarding, June 2022

We travel frequently except during the pandemic years 2020 and 2021. We took a family vacation in Beijing, Guilin, Xi'an in China, and Hong Kong.

Great Wall, Beijing, China (From left) Lynton's sister Vanessa, her husband Jan, Lynton, me, Will's mom Kathy, Mercy, and Will

Beijing National Stadium (Olympic Stadium)

Tiananmen Square, Beijing, China

My sister Yolanda's family (left), son Enoch, Yolanda, husband Patrick, and daughter Eva in Hong Kong

Lynton and I went to Germany, Austria, Spain, Anchorage in Alaska, Maui in Hawaii, Key West in Florida, and a short cruise to Ensenada in Mexico. We also took brief trips to San Diego, Santa Barbara, Las Vegas, and many nearby beaches.

Eagle's Nest, Bavarian Alps, Germany

Johann Strause II Statute, Vienna, Austria

Toledo, Spain

Maui, Hawaii

Starting in 2014, I attended Osher Lifelong Learning Institute with classes held at California State University, Fullerton. They offered classes to semi-retired and retired individuals. I have taken watercolor painting, drawing, poetry, various writing classes, and chorale.

Solitude

Mother-Daughter

As far as my hobbies, I enjoy gardening the most. My new summer project is to raise monarch butterflies. I raised about 20 butterflies in 2021 and raised about 50 in 2022.

Tea Rose

Hibiscus

Male Monarch

I'm grateful for the kindness of my family and friends during my time of need. I know there is no way I can repay them, but I know I can Pay It Forward and let the kindness repeat.

Kindness Repeats

Life has ups and downs
Friends will stay around
While the outlook bright on good days
Who knows what's ahead?
When you're half dead

Promising scenes fade away

The kindness of heart
Brought you a fresh start
Real friends hard to be found
Only wisdom knows
What tomorrow holds
What goes around comes around

One's fate made a turn
Stumbled, fell, and churned
Drowning into the ocean's deep
You're right around
Sensed cries without sounds
Graciously kindness repeats

Acknowledgment

I want to extend my appreciation to the individuals in the Writing with Feedback group at Osher Lifelong Learning Institute at California State University, Fullerton. My sincere gratitude for their honest and positive comments and suggestions. They assured me my story is inspiring and my writing is tight. They encouraged me to express my pain, worry, and fear during my journey, not merely the facts and statistics.

I'm grateful to my editor Larry R. Macklin for paying attention to the details and for his keen eyes to catch my errors. I appreciated his valuable suggestions to make my ideas clear and have a smooth flow in my written communication.

I'm in debt to my support group during my treatment. Jolyn Dawson stepped in to help me. She invited people to sign up to provide me with rides to my doctor's appointments and bring meals to my home twice a week. I was so touched by Sharon and Ken Rockwell for their consistent support of rides, meals, and emails, and offered to do anything to help. I was grateful for the generous support from Laura and Herb Turner in providing me with rides, ongoing email support, and even offering to clean my house. Laura brought me a can of protein powder, knowing I couldn't eat too much. When I felt better, she took me out for lunch. I'm grateful to the late Dr.

John Sailhamer to translate the Bible Psalm 1 directly from Hebrew and handwriting it for me, even though he suffered from Alzheimer's disease. I want to thank Mary Aposhian, Sue Sailhamer, Sally Monken, Christy Neynaber, and Rhonda Sittig, for taking me to the doctors and bringing me meals. I'm thankful to the members of my Joint Heirs fellowship group for their frequent get-well cards and emails. I appreciated Jenni Key and Diane Freeman for their multiple handmade cards with beautiful designs and encouraging messages.

Please forgive me if I didn't mention your name. Your kindness will be rewarded in heaven.

Aso by Miriam Hurdle

Songs of Heartstrings: Poems of Gratitude and Beatitude

Songs of Heartstrings: Poems of Gratitude and Beatitude is a poetry collection that includes nine themes. Each theme covers various aspects of Miriam's life experience. The poems are inspiring to the mind, heart, and spirit. The readers will resonate with these experiences. Hurdle illustrates the poems with her photograph and watercolor paintings.

Tina Lost in a Crowd

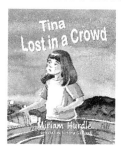

Tina Lost in a Crowd is about Tina who invited her friend Erica to attend a popular Tchaikovsky's Spectacular outdoor concert with her parents. It tells what the girls did after they got lost during the intermission. The story serves as a springboard for the adult-children discussion.

About the Author

Miriam Hurdle is a member of the Society of Children's Book Writers and Illustrators (SCBWI). Miriam writes poetry, short stories, memoir, and children's books. Her publications include the poetry collection *Songs of Heartstrings* and the children's book *Tina Lost in a Crowd.* Her poetry collection *Songs of Heartstrings* received the Solo "Medalist Winner" for the New Apple Summer eBook Award and achieved bestseller status on Amazon.

She earned a Doctor of Education from the University of La Verne in California. After two years of rehabilitation counseling, fifteen years of public-school teaching, and ten years in school district administration, she retired and enjoys life with her husband in southern California, and the visits to her daughter, son-in-law, and granddaughters in Oregon. When not writing, she engages in blogging, gardening, photography, and traveling.

To learn more about Miriam, please visit

https://theshowersofblessings.com

https://twitter.com/mhurdle112

Made in the USA
Middletown, DE
15 October 2023

40768875R00086